3000 800
St. Louis Community C

D0422712

LAW IN A LAWLESS LAND
MICHAEL TAUSSIG

Also by Michael Taussig

Defacement
The Magic of the State
Mimesis and Alterity
The Nervous System
Shamanism, Colonialism, and the Wild Man
The Devil and Commodity Fetishism in South America

LAW IN A
LAWLESS LAND

Diary of a *Limpieƶa* in Colombia

MICHAEL TAUSSIG

THE NEW PRESS

NEW YORK
LONDON

Published in the United States by The New Press, New York, 2003
Distributed by W. W. Norton & Company, Inc., New York

LIBRARY OF CONGRESS CATALOGING-IN-PUBLICATION DATA
Taussig, Michael T.
Law in a lawless land : diary of a limpieza in Colombia /
Michael Taussig.
  p.   cm.
Includes bibliographical references.
ISBN 1-56584-863-2 (hc)
 1. Violence—Colombia.   2. Paramilitary forces—Colombia.
3. Death squads—Colombia.   4. Terrorism—Colombia.   I. Title.
HN310.Z9V5763   2003
303.6'09861—dc21   2003051324

The New Press was established in 1990 as a not-for-profit alternative to the large,
commercial publishing houses currently dominating the book publishing industry.
The New Press operates in the public interest rather than for private gain, and is
committed to publishing, in innovative ways, works of educational, cultural, and
community value that are often deemed insufficiently profitable.

The New Press
38 Greene Street, 4th floor
New York, NY 10013
www.thenewpress.com

In the United Kingdom:
6 Salem Road
London W2 4BU

Composition by dix!

Printed in the United States of America

2   4   6   8   10   9   7   5   3   1

Limpieza, f. 1. cleaning. 2. cleanliness; cleanness. 3. purity; chastity. 4. integrity; honesty. 5. skill; ability. 6. clean play; fair play (in games).—*l. de bolsa,* (coll.) poverty, penury; *l. de corazón,* honesty, integrity; *l. de sangre,* racial purity; *l. en* or *a seco,* dry cleaning; *l. étnica,* ethnic cleansing; *l. general,* spring house cleaning.

Simon & Schuster's International Spanish Dictionary, Second Edition, 1997

Only the person who has measured the dominion of force, and knows how not to respect it, is capable of love and justice.

—Simone Weil, *The Iliad, or, The Poem of Force*

CONTENTS

AUTHOR'S NOTE   xi

THE FIRST WEEK   1

     MAY 5   3

     May 6   7

     May 7   13

     May 8   19

     May 9   35

     May 10   51

     May 11   65

     May 12   89

     May 13   103

THE SECOND WEEK   109

     May 21   111

     May 22   121

     May 23   145

     May 24   155

     May 25   161

     May 26   171

     May 27   181

POSTSCRIPT, NEW YORK   187

A VIEW FROM THE OUTSIDE   191

NOTES   203

ACKNOWLEDGMENTS   207

AUTHOR'S NOTE

In May 2001, I spent two weeks in a Colombian town taken over by paramilitaries imposing law and order through selective assassinations—what Colombians call a *limpieza*. I thought it would be useful to publish my diary of those two weeks, bearing in mind that I first visited this town as an anthropologist in December 1969 and have visited it almost every year since then. But as I typed up my diary notes I realized I had to fill out many ideas and references so that, although the diary format remains, it has allowed me to branch out in unexpected directions, including a perusal of the very idea of a diary and its relation to violence.

There have always been paramilitaries in Colombia's troubled history, or at least its modern history. This is not surprising given that the term itself is as elusive as what it points to, namely soldiers who are not really soldiers but more like ghosts flitting between the visible and the invisible, between the regular army and the criminal underworld of killers and torturers that all states seem to have no trouble recruiting when their backs are up against the wall.

The most recent resurgence of paramilitaries on the Colombian scene dates back to the mid 1980s, when men of means decided the national army was inept at defending them and their lands from the left-wing guerrilla and so formed their own police and armies which, being irregular, could fight a war of terror so terrible that peasant support for the guerrilla would evaporate. They have tripled in number since 1998 to an estimated 11,000 troops, control key cities in northeast Colombia, including Barrancabermega, Santander, and Cúcuta, and are a potent presence in the ports of Buenaventura and Tumaco on the Pacific coast. Like the guerrilla, they depend a great deal on the drug trade to finance their operations, which are made all the more sinister by the thinly concealed secret every bit as important as drugs: namely, that they are the clandestine wing of the army and police. Thus they lie beyond the reach of law, human rights, and the restrictions imposed by the U.S. government on its aid to the Colombian armed forces. Even worse—far worse, in my opinion—is that the paramilitaries also have the tacit support of many honest and honorable citizens of the republic who are fed up with corruption, the guerrilla, and street crime, it being street crime that, for many years, has been far and away the leading type of murder in murderous Colombia.

The classic scenario of paramilitary terror until recently was the arrival in an isolated village of SUVs with uniformed men carrying modern weapons. They would scrutinize a list of victims, sometimes on a laptop computer, round them up, torture, and kill them, often with machetes or the peasants' own chain saws, and leave the bodies suspended in public view before they drove off. As a result there are at least 2 million displaced persons in Colombia, a country of 43 million people.

However, by mid-2001, when I was keeping my diary of the *limpieza,* the paras not only indulged in spectacular massacres of defenseless villagers, but came to towns and stayed there, leaving the town to watch with bated breath, to wonder who would be assassinated next and how to make sense of what was going on.

Only after I showed my diary to Maria del Rosario Ferro, a young anthropologist in Colombia, was I made aware of the ambiguity of this word, *limpieza*. Sure, *limpieza* as "cleansing" now means to wipe out and kill defenseless people, much the same as a "purge" of the unclean. But, she pointed out, it is also used—and has a far older history—in healing a person or a home from malignity due to spirit attack or sorcery. Such healing not only neutralizes deadly force, but enhances a sense of self in place and time. Perhaps my diary plays on this ambiguity: that in the process of recording and detailing this new kind of *limpieza*, the diary might conserve this older sense as well, displacing the malignity of the events it describes. I certainly hope so, and now, looking back, thanks to her insight, believe this to be the reason for having written this diary in the first place.

THE FIRST WEEK

MAY 5

A BOMB EXPLODES OUTSIDE A CALI HOTEL, El Torre. No group claims authorship. Twenty wounded. This will be followed during the month by bombs in Medellín, Barancabermega, and in Bogotá close to the National University, where people are killed by a clever trick. First, a small bomb explodes. A crowd gathers. Police, explosives experts, and their dogs arrive. Then a much larger bomb explodes, killing them. There are no explanations for any of these bombs, not even an attempted explanation. The newspaper article I read on the Cali explosion describes things in close detail, repeats itself several times with variations, but never once ventures an explanation. It is an event from nowhere. This makes for mystifying reading, as you get absorbed in details and lose track of the burning question: Why has this been done? Who has done it? You are meant to figure it out for yourself like the crossword from the crisscrossing clues because this puzzle could one day mean your life. Like inkblot tests, each person reads a meandering logic into the event their own way. Might we say, might we conclude, therefore, that there are no explanations? Just notes?

I see Angela leaning forward on her chair before rushing off to a meeting of expectant mothers in the toughest slum south of Cali. She smiles wide, arms outstretched. She is smiling because she is a genuinely upbeat and generous person, but even more because she wants me to understand: "The war in Colombia? It's crazy. It makes no sense whatsoever. *¡No tiene sentido!*" There was a time, let me add, there used to be a time, when we believed. There was good and evil and the guerrilla was on the side of the angels. But the angel is now telling you it's crazy.

The problem here is that calling something crazy can easily come across as a gasp of exasperation that in effect calls for greater efforts to find the underlying reason which, in words that still chill me, is commonly defined in local editorials and by political scientists as rational self-interest on the part of "political actors" or "violent actors." But what if Angie is right? In other words: we can construct a chronology of events, but what connects them?

Isn't it possible to get caught up in events and react without knowing why? Later on you look back and find a reason, if you want to, but that rarely does justice to the way you got caught in the first place. To write a diary is to scuttle between these two phases, action and reflection, without quite reaching either. A diary is unstable. It unseats its own judgments because it lives on time's traveling edge, lingering where meanings congeal in case they dissipate.

Let us take another look at this notion of "actors." In his memoir *Prisoner of Love,* based on his time with the PLO in Jordan in the 1970s, Jean Genet says he failed to understand the Palestinian revolution "because the occupied territories were only a play acted out second by second by occupied and occupier. The reality lay in involvement, fertile in hate and love; in people's daily lives; in silence, like translucency, punctuated by words and phrases." [1]

MAY 6

TAXI DRIVER IN BOGOTÁ is choleric at the U.S.-dictated fumigation of peasants' coca plants with herbicides in the Putumayo in the south of the country. Defends the peasant whom he sees attacked by both the state and the guerrilla. If the peasant owns two cows, he tells me, the state takes one, the guerrilla the other. If there's a third, it goes to the paramilitaries! It is not possible to protest in Colombia, he adds, because of death threats and kidnapping, and that's why the country is so screwed. *Ambición,* he flatly states, is the root of the problem. It makes me feel more secure to hear that judgment cast on humanity as we hurtle round bends on the highway looking down on the city. We at least know where we are going and have got the whole thing sewn up. Eucalyptus trees fragrant in the drizzle also bring comfort, a touch of pastoral innocence and upper-class life interspersed by corrosive slums of tar paper shacks, a moth-eaten donkey, and malnourished kids with red cheeks whipped shiny in the cold wind. Like pollsters, the taxi driver is in constant contact with public opinion, which he also helps create. By turns funny and serious, he enters into his subject matter as well as maintaining his distance. What's more, he performs a valuable service in getting us from here to there in the closeness of his cab, linking us to the Great Unknown by means of the knowledge of the collective soul we credit taxi drivers.

Stranger intimacy. A wondrous thing. I once blabbed my secrets to one of these taxi drivers. Butter in his hands. It's quite the opposite of received opinion whereby the passenger milks the driver. Rumor has it that more than half of the taxi drivers are spies for the army. Rumor also has it that taxis are where you stand an excellent chance of being mugged or kidnapped, so people resort to radio-taxis, using secret codes in collaboration with the dispatcher over the telephone. But what's to stop the dispatcher from organizing a kidnapping, or some group intercepting the calls? I must put a stop to these runaway thoughts kidnapping my soul. But is not the cab a microcosm of life here?

I visit the book fair in Bogotá; an oasis of freedom and gaiety in the heart of this torn country. It extends for what seems like miles, attracting huge crowds. Who would have thought a book fair could have such an effect! People stroll as if walking through a park, meet friends, drink coffee, thumb through books and magazines. And not only middle-class intellectuals, by no means; people of humble origins and their kids as well. Vision of a new Colombia. How would our political scientists measure, much less explain, these "actors"? It seems here we have an equation: books equal peace.

NORMS OF CONDUCT. Headlines in Sunday's *El Espectador* on how the paras are imposing their morality in towns on the Atlantic coast; no earrings for men, no gay beauty contest, no miniskirts for women. Later I hear of paramilitary prohibitions of long hair for men, of wearing baseball caps backwards, as well as a curfew backed up by systematic assassination of *delincuentes*. Figure out how these things hang together and you have the solution to the whole puzzle.

What exactly is a *delincuente*, anyway? There's the English language equivalent, *delinquent*, but that sounds sort of pussy compared to what the word is meant to evoke in Colombia, which is closer to *murderous thug*, the word *thug* itself being a colonial import into English from India carrying all manner of specters and horror. And this raises the essential point, that the task words for crimes and criminals are generally cloaked in a curious argot and hence a deliberate obscurity, picking at the halo of transgression surrounding the criminal. The word *delincuente* in Colombia, today, beckons to a very wide *range* of crime, from pickpocketing to murder, as carried out—and this is crucial—by young people in roving gangs. The ambiguity is important.

"Whenever I write anything I ask myself how Castaño is going to react," a Bogotá journalist tells me. (Carlos Castaño is leader of the largest group of paramilitaries, known as the AUC.) "But," she goes on to say, "most journalists in Colombia are killed for exposing corruption." And plenty are killed. Right now Colombia is the most dangerous place in the world to be a journalist. I keep thinking of her fingers poised on the keyboard. The words being sorted out, waiting.

When I say Castaño is leader of the paras, I should explain that there are lots of different sorts of paras that grow out of local circumstances and are not necessarily formalized. There is the local merchant—say, the butcher—who decides to go on a killing spree at night along with his drunk buddies in the pickup or SUV—the favored vehicle of death squads in the Americas—so as to take out a few *transvestis* downtown, some *rateros* in the barrio, or the glue-sniffing kids huddled under the bridge. There are also the goon squads assembled by large landowners, and all manner of local self-defense organizations, formed against the guerrilla many years, even decades, ago. Some of these are officially recognized by the government as legitimate . . . well, legitimate what? "Private security forces" now abound in Colombia, employing far more people than the national police force and army combined. A strange hybrid, paramilitarization drifts into an obscure no-man's-land between the state and civil society. Nevertheless, Castaño is undoubtedly the powerful leader of a national organization, the Autodefensas Unidas de Colombia, with its own Web site, colombia-libre.org. What could offer better credentials than an address in cyberspace?

An ex-colleague of Castaño has described how he wakes around midnight and taps away on his computer in the silent night hours, e-mailing his lieutenants till the sun rises over the beleaguered republic. New spooks for new times.

How can we grasp this mix of centralization and anarchy? Does the reality lie in a hodgepodge of local groups slowly absorbed by Castaño's or somebody else's national organization that has yet to perfect itself, like the early days of the Freikorps, which went on to become Hitler's SA in Nazi Germany? Similar to the Colombian paramilitaries, they fought because they were well paid, wanted revenge against the Communists, and were sorely aggrieved by what they perceived to be a fall in the nation's standing and moral fiber. But most of all, as Barbara Ehrenreich points out, they fought "because that was what they did," and she cites a Freikorps paramilitary: "We ourselves are the War. Its flame burns strongly in us. It envelops our whole being and fascinates us with the enticing urge to destroy." [2] But bands of killers like these do not always fit easily into national organizations, especially hierarchical ones like the army. Their inclination to cruelty, romance, and anarchy fits them better for what has been called "the war machine," which has few rules—or else keeps changing them. [3]

William S. Burroughs had it down long ago: speed, secrecy, limitless cruelty, and—more important still—the thought-form that best goes along with this and what he practiced in his writing; namely, cut-ups and collages reconfiguring the text-image repertoire of reality. This war machine resembles an animal yet also a supernatural being. It partakes of myth, creates new myths, and exists in a state of continual becoming. Above all, the war machine understands atmosphere: how to suspend reality, how to create the black hole. The South African writer J.M. Coetzee once called this the practice of "mythological warfare." We all know some part of this, but the war machine is where this knowing is stored as in a bank of world history.

Given that creating an atmosphere is crucial to the success of the war machine, it is curious how little attention is paid to the art and culture of paramilitary terror by human rights experts. The people who do pay attention, the real experts, are the victims who live this atmosphere in their dreams and blood, especially with regard to the empty spaces that hollow out justice. Knowing what not to know becomes not only an art of survival but the basis of social reality. Is this why Genet talks of silence, like translucency, punctuated by words and phrases, and finds in the diary-form of his memoir both its echo and response?

MAY 7

HALF-HOUR FLIGHT FROM BOGOTÁ, high in the Andes, cold and gray, to Cali, capital of the lush Cauca Valley, visible from the air as a mosaic of sugarcane fields carving up nature into shapes for which it was never intended. They say only twenty-two families own the whole lot, about 125 miles long and thirty miles wide, and that the sugar industry would be long bust if it weren't for the subsidies provided by the state, which is controlled by the same people who own the sugarcane. Hot and sultry, Cali is famous for the beauty of its women and as the birthplace of salsa. Women transform as they step from the plane. Semitransparent blouses and shorts so short you blush. Great flair by these goddesses on their motor scooters threading through traffic stuck at lights as helmeted soldiers guard bridges and overpasses looking down upon them. There is an unstated fear that cities all over Colombia could be isolated anytime by the guerrilla deciding to blow up roads and bridges.

My Cali anthropologist friend collects me and my traveling companion, Ramón, who, like me, lives in New York City.

We go to lunch at The Turks in downtown Cali. In my memory it was always crowded, with tables and people sprawling onto the wide footpath opposite the old bullring, with idlers and beggars steering their familiar way through the diners. But today there are no customers. Not one. The raucous days of the cocaine boom are over. The big cartels have gone under, and smaller, discreet ones have mushroomed in their place. Factories are closed. Apartment buildings stand empty. Unemployment figures are off the charts, as are homicides. In this restaurant I feel I'm on a stage set with a fake waiter and I must do my very best to act my part and not let the team down. (What team would that be?) Later, we drive up the mountains to get a bird's-eye view of the city, an antidote, as it were, to our sense of alienation, trying to see it whole, have it whole, confronting the city's enigmatic danger in the same way that eagles are said to stare unblinking at the sun.

The anthropologist's doctor friend advises us against visiting a town an hour south of Cali on the Pan-American Highway, as it is securely in the hands of the paras, who are likely to view a foreigner as someone working for a human rights or an environmentalist NGO and then . . . He leaves the sentence unfinished. He's young, from Bogotá, a specialist, in no way political or leftwing, and he tells me the regional association of doctors in and around Cali supports the paras and he daren't say anything that could be construed as political in the hospital where he works. What's more, the paras are infiltrating the administration, faculty, and students of the local universities. They have carried out assassinations in universities in Medellín and on the Atlantic coast. Like the young doctor, professors and students in Cali are now fearful of expressing their opinions on many topics. But the surprising fact to me—the astonishing fact—is that many Colombians, rich *and* poor, now support the paras. This has to be acknowledged and understood, I say to myself, over and over and over again. For people outside this situation, it's easy enough to condemn such support. Trying to understand it is a different matter.

Of course such "support" may turn out to be a shifting sort of thing, supporting "the lesser evil." Moreover, support implies choice. But how much choice does a person have? What a joke! If you're not supporting us, you're dead—or worse, someone in your family is. As I finish this thought, I turn around and ask myself: "If the paras represent the lesser evil, what is the greater evil? What is it that we are all so afraid of?"

Late in the afternoon, by meandering back streets with shadows lengthening, I talk with a retired judge who used to work in a town of 50,000 people one hour away. Now she is too scared to go back even for a visit. She has heard that the town's business-people called in paramilitaries to clean out the town, which, during the 1990s, suffered mightily from violent youth gangs. There have been roughly one hundred murders of so-called "delinquents" since February at a fairly constant rate of several per week, sometimes two to three per day.

But *¡En Colombia nunca se sabe!* ("In Colombia you never know the truth!") The judge ends many statements with this sentence. Lawyers I know in the U.S. like to talk in aphorisms and adopt a tone of world-weary compromise. But this judge talks rules and procedures, her face tilted to the sky, accentuating the planes of her face as she tries to explain to me the latest change in the nation's many laws, which change daily. The universe of right and wrong is territorialized by a grid of laws, and each law is numbered. The signs against smoking cigarettes in the airports have the number of the relevant law made prominent, as do the notices on TV warning against sex and violence in an upcoming show. The infamous and much-abused law against illicit enrichment, designed to break into people's private bank accounts to track unusually large deposits due to drugs, was always spoken of as "law 30," no less natural than a law of nature. But the numbers never fit reality—neither the reality of the human condition nor the reality of the subtle distinctions necessary to law. The grid slips. And so a new law is made, and the judge is kept pretty busy just keeping up. When I tell someone I am working on a project I call "Law in a Lawless Land," they laugh and exclaim, "Lawless?!"

The judge's brother fled the country with his family eight months back. He was a lawyer working in human rights in southwest Colombia, a region with more than its fair share of conflict between guerrilla and paramilitaries. When we spoke a year ago, before he fled, he described it as a struggle for "the corridor" for cocaine and heroin coming down the mountains in the center of the country to the mangrove swamps of the Pacific coast and thence by fast launches to Central America. As he talked, drawing maps on serviettes in the restaurant, the maps got more and more complicated: "You get stopped at the government roadblock here," he said, making a heavy mark on the fragile paper. "Ten kilometers further on, the paramilitaries have their roadblock," and again he scored the paper so it tore. "And at the bottom of the mountain the guerrilla have theirs." Another angry assault on the map. I emerge with a fistful of wilted serviettes, like a bouquet. His assistant asks me a lot about Australia, which is where I was born. She is preparing her exit, too.

I can't help wondering about these "corridors." Drug shipments are minute in weight and volume, and Colombia is a big country with a wildly variegated "territory." "Corridors" are potentially everywhere. To talk in such terms seems to me more to bolster one's self-confidence than to depict reality, to attach yourself to the state apparatus and territorialization, to mimic what one imagines the big guys are doing with what passes for strategic thinking. I have visions of movies in which uniformed intelligence officers in subterranean bunkers address the generals using pointers directed at large-scale maps, trying vainly to figure out a logic in the flux and reflux of war across the face of the land where all you end up with is a bouquet of wilting serviettes.

And this of course is what people like me are meant to do, too: find the underlying logic that will make sense of the chaos. Your disorder; my order. Find the paths through the forest and over the mountains. Talk their language. Determine their self-interest. Square it out into real estate called "territory." Then dip it all into a fixing solution like developing a photograph. But what

if it's not a system but a "nervous system" in which order becomes disorder the moment it is perceived? At that moment the
bouquet perks up, no longer just a wad of crumpled paper.

The judge lives in a ground-floor apartment that seems like a
modified garage with but one window looking onto a sad, lower-
middle-class part of town. She lives with her venerably ancient
mother and her sisters, one of whom is dying from cancer, lying
in a fetal position in a room with a large interior window butting
into the communal living space and kitchen. I cannot separate the
things she is telling me about the violence in the country from
this personal tragedy. For a long time her sister has been dying.
Over two years. The family comes from a remote mountain village for many years in the hands of the guerrilla. It perches on
cliffs looking over a hot valley way below, through which a green
river twists through stark ravines and doubles back on itself in its
effort to pierce the *cordillera* and find the sea. How different are
those ravines from the streets her window looks onto now? Her
brothers and sisters left the village to study law, and now, she tells
me, the village barely exists. I sit by the dying sister. She wants to
talk to me. They have told her I am a writer. But she cannot
speak. She makes sounds her nurse understands.

There is a phone call: rumor has it, in the small town where the
judge worked, the guerrilla are going to counterattack tonight
and expel the paras. I call a friend there. She says it's false. But
how can she be so definite? *¡En Colombia nunca se sabe!*

MAY 8

THROUGH CANE FIELDS RAINING AND GLOOMY, Ramón and I rode the bus on our way to the small town where the judge had once worked and where I had friends. The road is raised like a causeway and, from its height, through the bus windows, which are always closed despite the heat, you can see the cane stretching out flat on all sides like the sea. But when now and again you see the wooded skyline of a peasant plot in stark profile next to land laid flat for sugarcane, or when you see a grove of bamboos lonely and isolated in the middle of a field of sugarcane, you get an idea of how beautiful this astonishingly fertile valley must have been before the 1950s, when sugar plantations took out the peasants' farms. For these farms were nothing less than artificial forests. The peasants did not grow crops so much as trees. And what trees! The mighty red-flowering trees known as *cachimbos* provide the shade for the underlying cacao trees, plantain trees, banana trees, coffee trees, orange trees, lemon trees, avocado trees, guava trees, *chontaduro* palms, *guanábana* trees, papaya trees, *zapote* trees, and others I can't remember. Here they were, all these trees, all mixed together with no apparent plan, no rows or design, trees of all hues, shapes, and sizes, underneath which grew an abundance of medicinal herbs and plants used for wrapping, for packing, the making of brooms, thatch for roofing, and firewood—not to mention the side-plots for corn and manioc. This was three-dimensional farming, mimicking tropical rain forest, a brilliant ecosystem, and just as brilliant an economy, requiring no irrigation, no store-bought fertilizer, no pesticides, little labor, little capital, and a continuous, year-round income as the crop diversity assured produce every two weeks.

Some people were bought out willingly by the sugar plantations that were set up in the 1950s. Others claim they were forced to sell because the plantations blocked access or flooded their farms. Women tended to hang on to the land, while their sons were often eager to sell. And when the owner died, and the inheritors were many, often with different fathers and hence conflicting rights, it seemed better to sell the land than to continue farming.

Denuded of trees, the land was put to the plow, and sugarcane spread from one side of the valley to the other for the benefit of a handful of white-skinned Cali families. Irrigation ditches were dug, at first by hand, then by giant backhoes imported with government-subsidized loans, eliminating the need for wage-labor. Pesticides and herbicides were sprayed, also by machines, eliminating the use of women and children who had previously been paid to weed the cane. The insect and fungal ecology changed. For the first time in the history of the valley, the cacao trees fell victim to a fungus called "the witches' broom." The black towns became ghettos enclosed by walls of cane. In the 1980s, a massive paper mill was installed upstream, polluting the river that ran through town. Now automated factories with little need for unskilled labor, many of them multinational, are moving in because of state-declared tax-free zones called "industrial parks." History moves fast in today's Third World, and the landscape moves with it.

The town looks tired and neglected. Electric cables festooned with moss crisscross the streets in elaborate cat's cradles. Unpainted brick houses stretch drearily in all directions. There is nothing cute here. Along with the high-ceilinged homes of mud and bamboo, the sharply peaked red-tiled roofs buffering the sun have long disappeared, leaving flat-topped, hotter dwellings, and meaner spaces. They lasted well into the 1960s, those giant homes, and on a lost corner you might still find one leaning and swaying like an old barn on a derelict farm in the U.S. And where are the people full of restless energy who used to fill the late-afternoon streets, laughing and shouting? An old friend from here, now living in Cali, greets me with her finger to her lips as I begin to ask about the paras. Shh, she says, eyes wide. Here, you can't say anything! Forever the drama queen, I don't know how seriously to take her warning. Last time I saw her, two years ago, I started to ask about the "industrial park" for the tax-free factories that were just beginning to be built. Same reaction. Finger on the lips, tightly pursed. "Shh! In this town, you can't say anything!" But I always think the real silence—what people in the villages sometimes call "the law of silence"—is so silent, you don't know the other person is being silent.

"So! Why did they come?"

"Well, didn't Castaño say he'd send people to whatever community asked for help?"

I walk across the plaza with P., whom I have known almost three decades. Out of the side of her mouth she tells me two paras are sitting on a park bench, taking it easy. I look straight ahead all the way across the park, feeling eyes boring into my back. It is not pleasant to know you can't look around in your own park. She tells me the paras announced their impending arrival in February with messages to the church and the authorities:

The town needs to get 300 coffins ready.

Heads up! The priest better be ready to work overtime.

Nobody seems to have a clear idea of who they are, what they are, and what they want. Nobody knows what to do. People here are much too scared to confront them, organize against them, or join them. What's more, they seem to disappear and appear at will within the town itself, like phantoms. Their earlier tactic of appearing out of the blue in an isolated village, assassinating the inhabitants in grotesque ways, and then pulling out within hours or a few days has given way to this bizarre form of permanent occupation. What before was a silent attack across a rural landscape bleached by fear is now movement spinning in on itself like a child's top, emitting clouds of dust and confusion. It takes your breath away. Their statement seems clear: "You think we're ab-

normal? You think we're beyond the pale? You think we're illegal and the state should force us out? Fuck you! We're here for
the duration!" It takes your breath away.

Normality crumbles, all over again. There is no outside any-
more, just as there is no clear boundary between the paras and the
state, which is, I believe, the most crucial characteristic of the
war machine. The paras are part of the state. But at the same
time, they are separate and even opposed to it. Their coming to
roost in the town is but the latest twist to this artful confusion,
which gathers the mythic force of the lightning that strikes in the
wild beyond and holds it steady in the townships.

Some people say there are thirty. Others say fifty. Some say
fifteen. Who knows? Some call them paras, others call them
pistoleros, and still others call them *autodefensas*—short for the
AUC—the United Self-Defense Groups of Colombia. This
ponderous name, mimicking the world of state agencies, is the
one used by Carlos Castaño for his militia formed on the Atlantic
coast several years ago with the express aim of exterminating the
Colombian guerrilla, one group of which killed his father and
later his brother. In 1983, he spent the year being trained in a
course in Israel. "In truth," he is quoted in his biography, *Mi confesión* (published in Colombia, where it has gone into eight print-
ings in five months), "I copied the concept of armed self-defense
from the Israelis; each citizen of the nation is a military power."
The crucial result of his training was that he became a different
person: "I learnt to dominate and control fear," he says.[4]

M. comes to the house to welcome me and draws me aside to

tell me there are *pistoleros* here called in by the *comercio* (meaning the local businesses). There are about fourteen. He knows their chief, a white guy with a big tattoo on his right forearm. "Are we in danger?" I ask. "No! They are well informed who's a *delincuente*." "But might not they think I'm working for a human rights group?" He pauses as if this is the first time he's thought about it. Then comes what amounts to a decisive clarification: "They are . . . not paramilitaries! *¡Son de limpieza!* They are people doing a cleansing!" But P. disagrees emphatically. She says you can't be sure. But me? I don't even understand the categories, and I suspect neither do they.

Names make identity an issue: paras, *autodefensas, pistoleros . . . those people* cruising the town on motorbikes. At first, most people tell me they are simply killers—*pistoleros*—hired by the town's business elite. A friend expostulates: *¡No tiene nada de ideología!* They have no ideology whatsoever! By which is meant, so it seems, that they are not paras at all! Then what are they? Who are they? And what does such a question imply for the country as a whole if we don't even know with whom or with what we are dealing, carrying all these different names and stories of origins, all these question marks with tattoos riding around on motorbikes? Sometimes I think this multiplicity of names and uncertainty about which name fits is a reflection of the entangled causes in Colombian society from which this killing force springs. Other times it suggests that the issue of identity is irrelevant because we are in another zone of being that has no name other than force. Like the wind.

Where do they live? It would be so nice to be able think of

them as having a home where they take off their socks, go to the bathroom, watch TV, call up their mothers, and listen quietly late at night to the rumble of trucks and the barking of dogs. A young woman from the outskirts of town tells me the paras live in the old hacienda just out of town. Hidden by a long drive of palm trees, its decayed grandeur now threatened by spreading factories and the tiny houses of the expanding town, the hacienda was the center of political reaction and the ghosts of slavery. But M. tells me the paras live close to the central plaza in the Hotel Cupido, a nondescript one-story building with a bright green neon sign out front with a little cupid cute and fat pulling on his bow. A house of love, housing killers.

Their chief used to be a cop, M. tells me, a cop in the newly formed elite police force known as the CTI (Cuerpo Técnico y de Inteligencia), another one of these chilling acronyms. What's more, he was a bodyguard for one of the town's judges before he got fired for some crime. Some story!—yet not uncommon. Many of the paras are ex-cops and soldiers. You do your compulsory military service, learn how to handle weapons and how the system of corruption works, and then get discharged. You look for ordinary work. There is none. But then there's the paras. And they pay well. Nevertheless, it is hair-raising to think of the deftness of this move from being bodyguard to a judge one moment, and chief of the paras the next. Perhaps this is the magical transformation you would expect with the war machine, like the tales of bandits active around here at the beginning of the twentieth century, when the landlords returned at the end of the War of the Thousand Days to kick the black squatters off their farms. The most notorious of these bandits could never be captured. It is said he would change into a plant or a fruit, which brings to mind the forest-type agriculture that the landlords wanted to tear down to make way for pasture for cattle.

Like the paras, their enemy, the guerrilla pay well, too. But once you're in the guerrilla, it must be difficult to return to civilian life, whereas for the paras, well, aren't they always already civilian? When the guerrilla try to return to ordinary life, they are killed by anonymous forces. To be a guerrilla fighter is like being a priest, only more so. Once a priest, always a priest, they say. But a priest can leave the church and not be killed.

Now and again I ask myself what makes the killings occurring now different from earlier times? How do I know it's not the same old killings that have surged through the town in waves since the early 1980s?

It's a different form of killing, people tell me. They go on motorbikes with a list. Some say with photos and state I.D. numbers as well. They go to the marketplace, about six blocks from the central plaza, for example, and cry out your name. You turn around, and they shoot. M. comes in excited, telling me an acquaintance got out of the bus near his place last week and was approached by them, list in hand. "Are you so-and-so?" they asked. "Yes!" Killed on the spot.

How many times I will hear of this list. It separates the living from the dead.

They know so much. People marvel at how well informed the paras seem to be. I am later told this is probably because they have access to the files of the CTI police. But I suspect the files are woefully inaccurate, which does not mean they are not dangerous.

The young women next door tells me that when the man who killed her brother gets out of jail, the paras will be waiting there to execute him, just as they killed another prisoner a month ago. It is a standard practice, to make up for what is seen as too liberal a legal code in which there is no capital punishment and sentences are thought by many to be way too light.

It was a year ago that I heard of the killing of her brother in a pool hall at night at the end of town. He was killed with a knife in the back, premeditated murder, his mother tells me matter-of-factly. The murdered man's son has just come in the door. Short-cropped hair, sunken eyes, age about fourteen, he stands robotlike without the slightest response as his aunt tells me about two bodies found only a week ago trussed with barbed wire in the trunk of a car abandoned by the side of the road. "How they crammed those bodies in such a small space I'll never know," she says.

Things felt quite different the night before, when someone was telling me people were feeling more secure because fewer people were being killed. Isn't it always like this? There's an apparent lull, and everyone sees the world in a completely new light, like when the weather changes from foul to fair. Days of depression all of a sudden lift with hope, and you completely forget what it was like to be scared all the time, trying to act normal.

There is something like a public barometer of insecurity. How it functions is a mystery. It is erratic and unreliable yet all we have, so we cling to it. What's more, it affects what it is meant to merely reflect, and this is probably why it exists in the first place. My reaction to the news that "things are getting better," or "things are getting worse," is even more perverse than the barometer, because the more violence and horror, the more my work seems worthwhile.

LAUGHTER AND HORROR. There is a young woman age seventeen who helps in the store here a few hours a day. Small, with a round face, she is unmistakably from a highland Indian family. She comes from the south, in the mountains near the border with Ecuador, close by the lowlands of the Putumayo, where most Colombian coca is now grown. I ask her about the U.S.-forced aerial spraying of herbicides in the Putumayo. Charming and smart, she laughs and throws back her head as she tells me how it destroys everything! Then the peasants go back to growing coca again, even in the same fields! (I hear from others that if the plant is radically cut back just before or after spraying, it survives as before.) I don't know how to fathom this mix of genuine alarm and laughter. She finds the destruction due to the spraying genuinely funny. The U.S. doesn't know what it is up against.

A friend tells me that some of the *delincuentes,* the ostensible target of the *limpieza* collaborate with paras as informants. A lawyer who used to work in local administration tells me what he fears most are the *señaladores,* the informants who might finger you.

Just after sunset I walk outside to test the temperature. Although many people know me, how do I come across to the paras as anything but a suspicious character out of place? The streets are dark and deserted. Trucks and agricultural equipment roar down the narrow streets, caring nothing for people on foot. I meet an old friend on the corner with his girlfriend selling fried *empanadas* made of corn. Without my asking, he tells me the paras have arrived to *limpiar* the pueblo. I pretend a theatrical attack of nerves, converting my fear into a farce. He smiles and says not to worry, they have been brought by the *comercio* and they go around with a kid from the town who points out the bad guys. It's a horrible solution, he goes on to say, but to have the criminals wrecking the town and making everyone's life hell is worse.

He always wanted to be a bullfighter and would practice daily, taunting a pair of horns or bicycle handlebars propelled on a small set of wheels by a friend running toward him outside the bullring in Cali. But like so many young people here, his life has been on hold forever. Always smiling and enthusiastic, his head cocked to one side, he tended his bar and its scratchy old sound system playing vinyl records. But the bar, for years a lonely outpost in a darkened plaza, has been dying for lack of customers. Everything is frozen in place, ready for dancing couples or people with more in their pockets than the money to buy a soda. If someone orders a beer, he polishes the dust off the bottle as he proudly brings it to the table. It could be champagne. One night three years ago, walking home from the bar, he was robbed and almost killed by a bunch of hoodlums with a homemade shotgun. He wrestled the gun from his assailants, and they sped off on their push-bikes. Unlike most people, he took the case to law and identified one of the assailants. The case dragged on for months, until he was advised to go no further for fear of physical retaliation. With his faith in justice, he comes across as naive. Perhaps I do him an injustice. Perhaps it is an act. Or perhaps he is the stuff of which saints are made, unalloyed innocence. But his story is classic: the man betrayed by justice.

People who support the paras do so in good part because the Colombian state cannot protect them from anything, not just from the guerrilla. From murder to traffic accidents, kidnapping or being mugged for your tennis shoes, the state is powerless whether you are rich or poor. The dean of a prominent law school in Bogotá tells me his wife was assaulted in the street a month back. Her earrings were torn from her ears. The police apprehended the thief, whom she then identified. Now she has to make a formal denunciation but is too frightened to do so. She fears the accused will find a way to get back at her or her children. And imagine if you are poor, how vulnerable you are.

But that is only the beginning of the betrayal. Much worse is to come, for the very authority you might want to turn to for protection is likely to make things worse. Again and again over the years this sense of the law as worse than crime, the ultimate injustice, if you will, has startled me. It is an axiom of survival that you must never act as a witness or go to the law with a problem, because the law, meaning in the first instance the police, is likely to make you into a suspect. Even the police will tell you that, if you know them well enough. And this corruption is what both the guerrilla and then the paramilitaries largely grew out of, in my opinion.

In a sense, people have only themselves to blame, because they actually welcome the police acting unlawfully when they secretly or semi-secretly kill petty criminals. Glancing at my previous diaries I see that all through the 1990s I am being told about this; as when, in October 1998, an all-knowing friend tells me the not-so-hidden reason the previous mayor was dismissed was because he was adamantly against a *limpieza*. "Ha!" she exclaimed with obvious approval. "With a military mayor, this town would be clean [*limpio*]." Even more surprising to me was the way she talked about this, as if instead of being a putrid, criminal activity, the *limpieza* is a legal, even natural, state of affairs; a matter, if you like, of routine local government policy, much the same as waste disposal, street cleaning, or education. I exaggerate, but not by much. Indeed, this blurring of law with crime in the popular imagination is a diffuse phenomenon I find intensely strange and significant. I well recall her son struggling to satisfy my curiosity as to the status of his visa and other government documents necessary for entering Venezuela. They were forged—in Cali, I believe—but to him, forged papers and state-issued ones bore equal legitimacy. Or, if not equal legitimacy, they somehow belonged to the same family of things, like close cousins. Our conversation went in circles because he couldn't grasp what to me seemed so essential: that forged state documents were diametrically opposed to real state documents;

that the mark of the official is that it is unique and cannot be copied and it is this that makes the state the source and epicenter of authority.

Or the young farmer I bumped into midday in the plaza in 1998 who had spent a year in prison for trying to shoot someone. The victim actually went to the police and made an official complaint. I raise my eyebrows in surprise, given all I hear to the contrary. "No! No!" he says. "That wouldn't happen today. People would be too scared." The conversation switches to the gangs in his village, a couple of miles distant. Two gangsters were attacked. One was killed outright with one shot. The other received seven shots and is now paralyzed in a wheelchair.

"God! Who did this?"

"The police, of course," he snorted approvingly. "If they didn't do this, the situation here would be impossible. We wouldn't even be able to stand here talking on the street corner!"

What was particularly significant about this story was his dramatic view of prison. "When I see a bird in a cage," he told me, "I want to free it." When he realized he was going to be jailed, he built a cage, and when he was released, a year later, he burned it. "The worst thing in the world you can do to somebody," he says, "is deprive them of their liberty."

Many people in Colombia justify the *limpieza* by saying the Colombian legal code is too lenient. Punishments are seen as weak, and hardly anyone gets punished, anyway. Yet at the same time, think about this man's attitude to prison, and couple that to his approval of police assassination. I myself think the police did well to put my friend in prison. Such acts of justice are surprising, given the climate of cynicism about the inefficiency and corruption of the police. They force you to see the situation as ever so much more complex, especially when you take into account that there are newspaper reports in that same year, 1998, of courts of law just north of here coming up with prison sentences of thirty years or more for ex-police forming "social cleansing" groups assassinating "socially maladapted" persons. But then we have to confront another family of facts: that the police are said to be killing people as part of their job, and that people seem to generally approve of this. Is this what sets the stage for paramilitarization? Could it be that what happened to this town in February 2001, with the arrival of the paras, was that the police were no longer able to keep a lid on the situation, even with their secret and semi-secret assassinations? In any case, the crucial thing is that justice in the form of clandestine assassination had become the norm.

MAY 9

WAKE TO CHURCH BELLS. Bare feet on the mosaic tiles. At midday a police helicopter circles low over the town, low enough to read the number in black letters on its belly. Round and round it goes for fifteen minutes. Strange to be watched like that, yet the police so powerless. Just the noise of the big bird flapping.

Today I am told that Navajo, one of my favorites, is dead! El Indio Navajo was how people referred to him. He deliberately shot himself dead four months ago on Christmas Eve drinking with friends. All of a sudden he reached for his 9 mm pistol and . . . *bang!* One of the town's few whites, age about fifty, of Lebanese descent, he was a barber (who cut my hair once, and never again!), a bullfighter who fought cows as a clown in the annual *feria* in August—and last but not least a man who lived more in his fantasies of Hollywood Westerns than in reality. I remember him emerging out of the black night four years back in the town plaza when a small group of us were drinking on the sidewalk by the one bar that was open, it being past the time when most people felt safe enough to be out at night. He was on his push-bike wearing a red nylon jacket and a red baseball cap with REEBOK across it, a shotgun over one shoulder, a large flashlight in his belt, and a machete slung across his back. The hat was pulled over his eyes, obscuring his elegantly lined face. We offered him a shot of sugarcane brandy, *aguardiente,* and he explained he was being paid as a night watchman by the shopkeepers around the plaza. Warming to his story, he informed me that he had recently attended a training course in small weapons with the U.S. Rangers on a hacienda not far from here (which struck me as totally unbelievable). And last year, in a confrontation with a gang of hoodlums at night, he pulled out his revolver in such haste that he shot himself through a testicle. He shrugs. Silly Navajo, and I love him for his silliness.

He told me the mayor was going to appoint him *inspector de policía* in one of the surrounding hamlets, a dangerous post on account of the gang warfare raging there. I knew that from the previous *inspector* with whom I spent a lot of time the past twenty years, including the six years he spent as the *inspector* in his office consisting of a gray steel desk and, high on the bare brick wall behind the desk, a portrait of Simón Bolívar's contemporary Santander, "the Man of Law," as he is known in history texts, Bolívar presumably being "the Man of War." The desk was bare but for a battered book of law codes, many out of date. In the corner was a cement box for files, and presiding over it all was an exceedingly pretty teenager from the hamlet acting as secretary with her own portable typewriter, which she took home at night.

It was she who memorized the lengthy verbal formulae with which each declaration began. Her fingers flew across the keyboard quadruplicating copies on her tiny machine. But there was barely any paper on which to write. Months, maybe years, they'd been waiting for the government to get them paper. So the inspector used to solicit paper from the "enemy," the paper factory polluting the river, the same factory that distributes picturesque calendars in its name extolling the beauties of nature. This previous inspector has lived his entire life of seventy-plus years as a peasant out there. He knows everyone and everything and has miraculously survived three attacks on his life by gangs the past six years, in the last of which three young men had him on the ground out by the cane fields, fired a gun into his mouth, and left him for dead by the side of the road in the gutter. His "box" of false teeth saved his life, he says. The bullet is still inside his head.

I told Navajo it was too tough out there, but he laughed. "As long as you can get two locals to work with, you can go wherever you want, find out who the troublemakers are, and execute them!" he replied.

So, Navajo is a homeboy paramilitary! And also a lovely, decent, crazy son of a gun, with the most winning smile and enjoyable stories that surely, not even he, can take for real.

The mad poet Rubén tottered by; thirty-five years old and skinny as a rail, he lives off a derivative of cocaine called *bazuco,* which he buys with the few pennies he gets by writing poems on the spot for people and selling them. His whining and begging make people squirm, but not as much as when he turns aggressive and heaps scorn on the philistines when they reject his poems. *"¿Para que sirve?"* snarled Navajo. *"¡Ni por abono ni por tierra!"* "What's he good for? Neither fertilizer nor soil." I could not really believe he meant what he said. It was no less a spectacle than Rubén's; some sort of performance that Navajo indulged in when he had an audience, like when he did cartwheels over the cow's horns at the bullfight.

A year or so before the paras arrived here in February 2001, there was a large graffiti in white letters signed by the FARC guerrilla on the wall of the school opposite where I was talking with Navajo. It was a declaration of death to the delinquents of the town as well as the people who shield them (*alcahuetes*). (One of the things you constantly hear about is the absolute determination with which families—especially mothers—shield their "delinquent" offspring.) Navajo told me confidentially that this graffitti was not the work of the FARC guerilla, but of some locals using their name. For, like the paras, the FARC have a reputation for carrying out urban and small town *limpiezas*. Yet what he said surprised me. Given the reputation of the guerrilla, I did not think anyone would falsely use their name.

The locals could have eliminated a big bunch of *delincuentes* on this death-list, said Navajo, if only there had been more collaboration! He grimaced, then broke into a smile. He liked to flavor his speech with Arab words meaning (he said) "No!" or "big" or "dishonest." At least he said it's Arabic. He told me the guy who assassinated don Felix had been arrested and that he,

Navajo, was going to fix him properly. Don Felix was a mild-mannered man from a Lebanese family with a haberdashery in the central plaza. His son got into drug dealing and failed to pay off a debt, so the story goes. One day a man came and stationed himself in the plaza under a tree and waited till don Felix appeared at the doorway of his store late afternoon and shot him from across the street. A year later I was invited to lunch in the home of an aspiring video-maker ten blocks from the plaza. We sat in the sweltering midday heat in straight-backed chairs, the sort one associates with Spanish formality but never sees around here. My host had bought them from don Felix's widow, who abruptly had sold everything and left town. He told me he got them cheap.

Navajo kept looking up from our conversation at the young men walking past us as if they were criminals he was going to have to deal with soon.

I saw him by accident the following morning. It was a beautiful day, with a blue crisp sky. He invited me, half-awake, for a coffee. Asked me about President Clinton and told me Monica was paid to expose him. Shook his head regretfully, as is the way of the wise. "Don't you get tired," I asked him, "having to fight fifteen-year-olds all night?" He replied: "I am fifteen years old myself."

That was in 1998. Last time I saw him was in July 2000, late at night in the town plaza, slowly circling the plaza on his push-bike, wearing the same red nylon jacket and holding a machete, wrapped in newspaper, flat on the handlebars. He was still working—he said—as a night watchman but looked subdued. He had been recently attacked by "bandits" who'd stolen his machete and shot him in the back.

When I asked why Navajo killed himself, a friend placed his hand on his forehead and put his fingers in the form of a **V**, the horns of the cuckold.

Now and again I ask myself how the mad poet Rubén has not yet been assassinated? I remember not so long ago someone told me he wouldn't last till New Year's. You must think less of me for thinking this. Last time I saw him in May, his production had become more professionalized. Instead of scribbling poems on the spot and handing them over to you, he'd photocopied two sheets, folded over into four pages. The front was like a book cover and carried an illustration of a negroid face, lips and eyes accentuated, looming out of a swirling mist in which two tiny nude black human figures, male and female, were floating, reaching out for each other.

On the front of the pamphlet was the title:

Sleeping Mini-Series For A. and Other Shipwrecked Victims
Mini-Serie Dormida Para A. y Otros Naufragios
POEMAS

On the back of this mini-book:

"Poetry is the trace of love."

On the inside:

> *Always*
> *The Unique Work*
> *Of the Sun,*
> *Wheat,*
> *Water and Light,*
> *Is*
> *Poetry and*
> *Life*

So strange that Navajo, always wanting to kill killers, would end up killing only himself, while Rubén, a walking dead man furiously writing romantic poetry, is impervious to assassination.

Why a walking dead man? Because a character such as Rubén is the archetypal victim of the Colombian *limpieza*. He scares many people, I guess. The very name, the *limpieza*, "the cleansing," says it all. There is a name for such characters, *desechables*, and it means "throwaways."

* * *

Before the arrival of the paras in February 2001, which is when public assassination in broad daylight got under way, assassinations of such persons were more sporadic and secretive. Trying to collect statistics on homicide in August 1998, for example, I got to know the new state prosecutor, D., and visited him in his rented room, where he would be watching his tiny TV hours on end in this town he didn't know, dirty glass panel above the door, cheap curtains on the window looking onto the dark patio. Like the CTI policeman living in the same house, D. was white and from the state capital. It had not passed without comment that there was something amiss in having law enforcement people from another cultural and geographic area who would be slow to grasp events here. The town has five state-appointed prosecutors known as *fiscales,* each one with a staggering burden of some 300 to 400 cases pending and no assistants. In 1997, for instance, police records indicated 105 murders, but the court processed no more than 12 that year, and I would be surprised if more than one of those reached sentencing.

D. was new to the job, and nervous. He had reason to be, because a prosecutor is a key link in the chain of officials bringing a case to trial and is therefore subject to bribery and violence. It was eight o'clock at night and a call came for a *levantamiento,* meaning a state examination of a dead body at the scene of the crime. "Do you want to come?" he asked me. I declined, not wanting to be involved in more horror after reading autopsy reports all day and feeling awkward at getting so close to the law. Then I impulsively changed my mind. After all, this is what anthropology is all about, isn't it? Getting into unpleasant situations, including other people's business, where you have no right to be? A science, after all.

As I get my camera and notebook, D. hurries out to buy a handful of cigarettes. An unmarked and decrepit station wagon filled with CTI police *put-puts* to the door, and we churn off. I see my friends W. and M. standing in a dim light on the corner by the plaza, but I do not wave or shout a greeting. In fact, I feel I no longer know them. I have joined with an alien power and have severed my connections with them, with the pueblo, and even myself. Now I'm with the law. I feel a surge of power.

W. looks hard at the car. He doesn't see me. I see this same concentrated look on the faces of other people on many of the street corners we pass. Our car has no sign saying it's a state vehicle, and here, especially at night, your life may depend on correctly identifying each car and knowing what it is up to.

We roll along the road to Cali with dreary cane fields on either side, then turn after ten minutes onto a dirt road that leads to an abandoned sugar mill. A light by the main road indicates a watchman. Otherwise, the darkness of the cane presses in like covering your face with your hands. Along the dirt road in the cane field we see a red light and fallen trees pulled onto the road. Two police are there with a motorbike. They give me a suspicious look. We park the car with the headlights shining on the body by the side of the road. Twisted. Misshapen. Lying face-down. Green dirty shorts of a light, cheap, clinging material, unraveling around the left leg. White tennis shoes. A dirty bandage around the left forearm. No shirt. Something clenched in his right fist. Running down the back is a curved, well-defined line of dried blood. Most striking of all is that his back looks more like his chest, the way it sticks out and the way the ribs flare. This is a body that could have been thrown with considerable violence off the back of a pickup.

When we arrived, a portly CTI fellow who had a black bag on his lap in the car, put on a dirty white lab coat with an insignia on it—national something or other—and started to take photographs. But the flash didn't fire. I thought of offering my services, but decided I best keep in the background. He put on dirty surgical gloves and started to "pick" at the corpse, trying to get an idea of how many bullet holes there were; one through the chest, from the front, they said, a small hole on both sides of the skull and a huge crater in the temple.

"*Vicioso,*" they keep saying. "Druggie."

"*Vicioso.*"

The other CTI guy, also a white man, had put on rubber gloves, too, and was slowly poking a stick into a pool of coagulated blood like a child finger-painting.

Lightning flashed. Now and again, thunder rolled. There was a wavy line of light on the horizon of the western sky. Acrid smell of smoke from the town on the other side of the drainage canal. Silhouettes of low-roofed houses. Every now and then an eighteen-wheeler truck loaded with cane would roar past, lights beaming through a fog of night and dust.

One of the motorbike police—also white—glares at me and asks D. who I am. His companion, an Indian, seems scared. The first cop has a Galil over his shoulder. I have a feeling there is more going on here than meets the eye. It dawns on me that maybe the cops are the ones who killed the *"vicioso,"* and this is an elaborate charade.

The portly CTI guy still has his gloves on. He lifts up the left arm and undoes the bandage while lecturing D., telling him that these *viciosos* often use a bandage like this to hide *baʒuco,* a cheap derivative of cocaine, or to use as a shield for knife-fighting. Sounds like a cop trying to sound like a cop. They treat D. with outward signs of respect. He's an essential part of the act even if he doesn't yet know it. I like D. and feel sorry for him.

They open the right hand. There is a brown-paper packet held tightly. A ripple of curiosity runs through our group, and we gather closer. It contains tiny packets like fish scales containing *baʒuco.* They are called *cienes,* the portly fellow tells us— "hundreds"—on account of their costing a mere one hundred pesos (about seven U.S. cents). More and more I get the feeling this is a setup. That the packet is a plant. But then, why all the bother? Is this what "law" means, this theater?

All this time one of the women in our group is sitting in the station wagon filling out a printed form in pencil. The other woman is the portly fellow's girlfriend come along for the ride. He says there's no more to do. His flash doesn't work. We should drop the body at the hospital morgue. With his buddy he slips the body into a plastic bag. "Careful! It's my last one!" They slide it in the back of the station wagon, with its tennis shoes sticking out. So incredibly sad, this twisted body with its hand full of fish scales. The end of the road. The story of coca.

Nobody here has a clue who the dead man might be, because nobody in the CTI—the Corps of Police Intelligence—knows anything about this town or region. They keep saying they wish Alonso were here, because he knows everyone.

Body crunched into the back, we drive off. I am but a couple of inches from our cargo. We drive to the back gate of the hospital.

Kids zoom out on tiny bicycles. Even though it's late and we are in a sparsely settled part of town on the other side of the river to the town center, these kids smell death and love to ogle and get close to it. The two cops drive up on their motorbike and get the watchman, who turns up with a bunch of keys and a revolver sticking out of his belt. One of the CTI guys suddenly says we should take the body to the cemetery—not the main cemetery close to the center of town, but the cemetery where the marginal people are put, the *cementerio laico*, the "secular cemetery"—because the hospital has no refrigeration for corpses and you can't leave an N.N. (anonymous person) for two weeks in such a state. The body will decompose, and N.N.s tend to be diseased and dangerous, he says. Even in death—especially in death—this man is frightening.

As we drive through the almost deserted streets, I see people staring at us through curtained windows until we reach the end of town, where a man with a withered leg walking adroitly with a crutch comes out as soon as we stop. He has long hair and slurred speech. He opens the gates, and the station wagon slowly squeezes through with barely an inch on either side. People start to gather as the black bag is withdrawn. They push and shove and ask to see the face. *"¡Es negro! ¡Tiene tenis!"*

The bag is put on a slab in a small shelter with unlockable doors. There is an unstated feeling that it would be disrespectful of the corpse, even of such a one as this, to leave it to the rats and the spirits of the cold night air. And who are we in our unmarked station wagon passing through deserted streets with our white-jacketed, rubber-gloved crew having just dumped a crumpled body on a slab in the *cementerio laico* at the end of town with a ghoul guarding the gate? Who are we? A man keeps circling around, trying to get a better look at me. What does he want? Now I know how the *fiscales* must feel.

I come home bombed-out and sit on the plastic couch staring at the yellow wall without saying anything for half an hour. P. offers me a drink, which is a rare thing as there is not enough money in this household to buy liquor. But neither of us move. I guess it's the first time—one of "one such"—that I've really felt the meaning of violence, and felt both terrified and deeply sad for Colombia—this twisted, dirty, almost naked body in its sticky, dirty pool of blood clutching at its fish scales.

Next day I find out the dead man is "The Boxer" and that, according to many people, he was a *bazuco* addict—a *vicioso*—who, half out of his mind most of the time, would walk disheveled through town boxing with imaginary opponents, his fists flailing the air. People get to fear and hate *viciosos* like rabid dogs, same way they get to hate the barrio of squatters at the far end of town. They want to exterminate them to the last pathetic one. Yes!

Looking back over these notes scribbled down at the time, I ponder over the frankness, the naiveté, and the imprecision. What does it mean when I write to "really feel" and just what is "the meaning of violence"? What does it mean to reflect on these things as opposed to feel them? And why, given all the terrible things that come my way—why would this particular event stand out so? My guess is that it's not "violence" per se—whatever that means—but experiencing violence transfigured by the law absorbing the violence and magnifying it.

In a famous passage, Nietzsche suggests that criminals become hardened by observing that they and the police use the same methods, except with the police, the methods are worse because the police excuse their actions in the name of justice. What sort of methods? "Spying, duping, bribing, setting traps," says Nietzsche, "the whole intricate and wily skills of the policeman and the prosecutor, as well as the most thorough robbery, violence, slander, imprisonment, torture, and murder, carried out without even having emotion as an excuse." Nietzsche helps me understand why the violence of the law sickens me more than the violence of the criminal, and why P. and I sit like stone beyond help in the stillness of the night. Nietzsche helps me understand how the violence of law is not only a question of guns, handcuffs, and gaols, but, far worse, what gives that violence its edge and its lip-smacking satisfaction is deceit in the service of justice. What I witnessed and, indeed, took part in, seems to me to have been just this charade. The fact that I can't be sure seems to me part of the deal. And the fact that I call it a charade should make one weep tears of joy because it suggests I still hold out hope that justice is sometimes something more than a charade. What I was part of was automatic and routine, but also ad hoc and made up as it went along. Each time must be different. Sometimes the flash works. Other times it doesn't. Just as the Boxer was visible punching the sky in ragged clothing, too visible, too flashy, so the law cruises the slipstream of traps sprung after night falls and the Boxer lies there without his photo being taken, just a memory, a memory of a tent-shaped bundle of bones strapped to its tennis shoes in the middle of the cane fields.

One question remains, however: If Nietzsche puts us on the right track, is it so surprising that the paras and the police are virtually the same? No wonder D. suffers from *nervios*. I would like to think the problem Nietzsche poses about the police being always already criminals is "merely" philosophical, indeed densely theological and ultimately insoluble in those terms. I would like to think there are more practical ways of getting at this problem.

*   *   *

The murder of the Boxer—I can still see the image I was given of him walking stiff-legged along the street punching the air and talking to himself—was but one of several different ways death was assigned before the paras came and installed themselves in February of this year, 2001. I think the first I heard of the paras as a name to contend with was late one afternoon in October 1998, when I visited one of my oldest friends, named L., sitting in the gloom of her home, a candle burning in front of a religious image in the bedroom. Slowly, her tired husband, C., got up to buy a Pepsi from the corner store for me and Jorge, whom I had just run into on the street. In a hushed voice, L. told us—having first closed the front door—that two bodies had been found in plastic bags by the side of the main road outside town and that one of them was a relative of a friend of mine. She said it was the *autodefensa* who were responsible. The word—*autodefensa*—is awkward on her lips. People say there were three strange cars: a red one, a green one, and a black one. Like a fairy tale, I think to myself. A man was on his way to work and the red one stopped him, asked the way to the neighboring town, wheeled around, and sped off. Jorge interjected at that point to relate how when he was walking to work at six in the morning, a red SUV stopped and hailed him. He shivered with fear—that's how you get killed now, by crazy people who use you for target practice, he says. They asked him for the *"vía central,"* a term foreign to these parts, and accelerated away. L. shook her head sadly and knowingly, although truth to tell, I think she enjoys these tales. But then, who doesn't?

On the street we meet F., a young white woman who sells Avon beauty products out of her home. "No!" she says, when we bring up the recent killings, "that's not *autodefensas.*" *"Eso se llama . . . para . . . paramilitares."* (That's not *autodefensas.* That's . . . para . . . paramilitaries.) As an afterthought, she adds: "I have a friend who is paramilitary." It is 1998. We are learning a new language. And we are learning that one's friends have friends who are killers.

MAY 10

I WAKE BEFORE DAWN to a phantom world and draw tight the thin blanket where I sleep in the back of the house by the kitchen. Cocks crow, shattering the darkness. This is the time when spirits gather, spirits of the dead, looking for a companion to take to the other side.

It takes twenty-five minutes in a taxi to get to the once picturesque hamlet by the river where my ex–*inspector de policía* friend lives. Ramón is with me, and I enjoy showing him the town's hinterland, which, for me, is like turning the pages of history. It is the first time I've been back in two years, because the *delincuentes* made it too dangerous. Long avenues of dust-clogged roads take us through the cane fields where the gangsters were said to hide, awaiting their prey traveling to and from the town. Now and again we pass a horse-drawn cart moving at a fast clip, full of people clutching their baskets with their legs dangling over the side. Otherwise there are no people at all. And no trees. Just the baking sun, the gray dust like fine soot churned up by heavy plantation tractors drawing trains of wagons for sugar cane, and on all sides cane fields planted over what was once home to people living on their forest farms. Here and there a tiny island of forest remains, weighed down by the dust, held captive to the cane pressing in on all sides. We come to a stop at one of these islands and greet the inspector, who lives alone in an adobe hut by the side of which in the shade is a gigantic pink pig with white tufts of hair, lying exhausted on its side. Chickens peck in the underbrush of this quarter-acre farm bursting to the seams with nature's bounty. No wonder the beautiful B. is here buying oranges and whatever else he's got for sale: mandarins, plantains, and bananas, too. But nevertheless, what a surprise. She used to be the telephone operator in the brick building a mile away housing the office of the *inspector de policía* and a never-used, decrepit jail. The building was hit by lightning a year back and the switchboard never repaired, so that while B. still lives in the *Inspección* with her small child, she now adds to her income as a *revendedora*, buying produce from peasants and selling it in the market on the western side of the valley in a town overrun by paramilitaries trying to control access to the western range of the Andes and thence the Pacific coast. Despite his seventy years, the inspector is atop a high tree harvesting oranges to sell to B. Plague of ants eating the farm, he tells me on his descent. Can take out a tree in a night.

Sitting on the cup of his kitchen hand-mill is a *guanábana*, which I sketch as we talk in the cool of the morning. A *guanábana* looks like a pineapple but is longer and has a milky green color. It grows on a tree and weighs several pounds. When you break through the skin you find sickly sweet white flesh surrounding lustrous black seeds scattered throughout. Early colonial artists in Brazil painted the *guanábana*—what a name!—as a symbol of the magic of the Tropics, beautiful yet eerie in its splendid difference, which overcomes me, too, as I sit here sketching it in 2001. Soft inside their armor-plated hides, it seems to me *guanábanas* are handled with a bit more care than any other fruit, like prehistoric freaks that have overextended their evolutionary time allotment. Only peasants grow them. They have yet to be appropriated by agribusiness.

He was inspector out here for six years in the mid-1990s. Despite the title, an *inspector de policía* is not attached to the police. He is more like a mini-mayor, a local peasant elected for a few years by the mayor of the municipality to serve as a jack-of-all-trades in state administration of one or two adjoining hamlets. The electricity bills for the inhabitants of the hamlet come to his office for distribution. The electoral rolls are compiled there. The courts in the municipal seat get him to serve their summonses. And, most important, he is often the first port of call for someone reporting a crime or a problem with a spouse or neighbor. It was inevitable that he would get drawn into the gang warfare raging between the different hamlets he was supposed to serve.

The gangs have disappeared, he tells us. The parents of several killers have evacuated their offspring as far away as Bogotá. He rolls his eyes. Standing stock-still in the middle of changing his sweat-drenched shirt in the patio, gray hairs curling on his chest, sharply defined shoulder muscles. "It was so, so, bad. . . . You have to be grateful to these *pistoleros*. . . . *Uno quiere trabajar honradamente. . . .* All you want to do is work honestly." Attacked three times in the past few years, he knows what it is to be violated. Before that he was active in the big strikes on the plantations in the 1960s, after which he was an organizer in the peasants' union, ANUC, and was badly beaten by the Colombian army ten years ago at night on the earthen floor of his hut.

I recall a conversation with him in January 1990, when he insisted the guerrilla was an absolute necessity. He called them "the army of the poor"—in contradistinction to the police and the national army, whom he called "the army of the rich." In his eyes, the landowning class wages a continual war against the peasant, very much including the Indians in the hills. It was the landlords, he told me, who some three years ago paid a professional assassin—a *sicario*—to kill the Indian priest in the nearby town. The priest was one of the first Indian priests ordained in Colombia, a killing that unleashed killings and kidnappings in retaliation by the Quintín Lamé guerrilla.

As for the name of that small and short-lived guerrilla outfit, Quintín Lamé was a long-haired, cheroot-smoking, Paéz Indian from the *cordillera Central* who led a memorable uprising against the white elite of Popayán in the early twentieth century. He was caught and sentenced to lifelong house arrest in an Indian reserve in the lowlands of Tolima. There was a photograph of him in the state archive in which I worked in Popayán. Full of youth, relaxed, and smiling mischievously in the middle of a bunch of police posing for the camera, his long hair, like a hippie's, flows into his cloak made of reeds. It rains a lot and is cold up there near the *páramo,* so you need protection, even if it's only a cloak of reeds.

I saw the photograph in the early 1970s and have never forgotten the smile or the cloak. It took more than half a century for the rebellion he led to recur, but this time it's unstoppable, which is one reason why the paras are so active in the mountains of this province as well as down here.

"There is no law! There is no law!" the inspector kept repeating. *"Para el pobre no hay ley. No hay ley! . . ."* ("For the poor there is no law. There is no law!") Like a stuck record. We were walking out to his place through the black cane fields, the stars so brilliant, the walls of cane, so dense.

> *Todavía creo en el amor*
> *y en la paz, también.*

Music on the bus leaving the town.

> *I still believe in love*
> *And in peace, too.*

Sometimes when you pass an open field that miraculously has no sugarcane in it, you might see a path zigzagging over the plowed furrows or through the weeds or whatever is being cultivated, maize or beans. It must be a peasant plot. The path is never straight.

Walking out to the inspector's place was still possible in 1990. There were no gangs in the countryside then. One night as I approached I heard salsa music filtering through the plantain trees alongside the road. It was coming from the little store made of mud and bamboo, just beyond the inspector's home. Five or six people were on benches with empty bottles of *aguardiente* in front of them on the concrete slab under the overhang, the owner leaning over the half-door working as DJ. There were two huge speakers at either end of the slab, with an old toothless couple dancing slow and smooth as silk. Two old women skinny as reeds were dancing with each other. Adolescent girls were watching, one in black nylon tights up to her neckline. These tights are referred to as *chicles,* or chewing gum, and these legs were surely the longest legs in the world. Wearing a short pink cape, huge white ringed earrings, her hair in tiny braids, she was sucking on a lollipop. More than likely she was a servant on leave from her job in the city.

My young companion from the town, Robinson, sat with me by one of the speakers, drinking a Coke. It was a moment frozen in time: the dark beyond the plantains, the scars of poverty and hardship on the faces of the people dancing, the grace of the movement that the space they made opened out.

They were strange, these moments, the way they linger, forever it must be. Going out on that road years ago late afternoon, I remember two young men, field hands, by a push-bike with a portable radio tied to the cross-bar. The shadows were long. Without a word they were dancing slowly in and around their shadows around the upright bike. We didn't say a word. Just us, the setting sun, the dusty road, the shadows.

The then-president of Colombia, Virgilio Barco, announced in 1990 that he wanted to pass a law banning war toys, as well as films, videos, TV shows, and magazines depicting violence. A week before, the sale of horse meat was decreed legal as another inspired presidential measure to relieve hunger. The inspector was indignant. "But the horse is noble! And useful to mankind! How could you kill a horse, the animal we poor peasants depend upon? Where is this country going?" he cried.

Looking back, it now seems as if during the 1980s and 1990s the ground was being prepared for the paras. The police here were visible and clean, but at night it was a different matter. Together with their friends they were killing *viciosos, rateros, transvestis* (drug addicts, thieves, and transvestites), and God knows who else besides. But not only the police! By no means! In fact, many people assured me the majority were revenge killings carried out by civilians on one another. This was the real criminal justice system, and everyone knew about it except me. Bodies were turning up all the time by the bridge. A friend was coming home late at night from a party in Cali and saw two guys dumping bodies there. They waved him on with pistols. It got so routine in the 1990s that people took little notice.

An ex-mayor, who never lost an opportunity to set me straight, told me at that time that Colombia needs a dictatorship and the authorities should assassinate 300 of the sons-of-bitches a day. As a young man he had been a member of the Presidential Guard in Bogotá. What with his tremendous height and ramrod-straight back, it was not difficult to imagine him in his shiny helmet, sword, and black uniform touched with the gold leaf of the Wars of Independence. It was said he himself had been a famous bandit, although at what time in history was never clear. Was it before or during La Violencia of the late 1940s and 1950s? And here he was advocating assassination of all bandits. He was loaded, absolutely loaded, with charisma, even when old and shaking with Parkinson's disease. Everyone respected him and, truth to tell, was a little scared of him, too. But they would never say so. They would say it was respect.

Ten years later, in 2001, here we are sipping the hot chocolate the inspector makes with his hand-mill from his cacao trees. We add the Cointreau I brought him as a present from my flight to Colombia. Fancy stuff. B. shudders as it goes down. We make plans to start up our own Cointreau business with the inspector's oranges that lie around us in burlap bags as big as ourselves. B. will be the saleswoman.

The inspector tells us how he spent his pension to cultivate a plot of his mother's a mile away. Everything was stolen. Now he has to sell that plot because it's impossible to farm if you're not living on site to ward off the thieves that are your neighbors.

6:30 P.M., back in town to discover that a twenty-eight-year-old man was killed last night in his store opposite the home of my old friend L. Killed by two *malandros* (criminals), they say, not by paras! L.'s daughter, age nineteen, is hardly able to talk, she's so excited. She knows the family well. "He told them, 'Take what you want, but don't kill me. Rice, *aguardiente* . . . take it all!' But they killed him with a bullet through the liver, in front of his children." "He didn't die straightaway," she adds. "He lived long enough to name his killers."

Rumor has it the paras are going to use bombs to drive people out of the squatter settlement at the end of town called Carlos Alfredo Díaz (CAD). It acquired that name from a student in the squatters' movement who was shot dead by police some twenty years ago, during the occupation of a mere three acres of sugarcane plantation land to house the homeless. Since then it has acquired a sinister reputation that seems to me way exaggerated, even ludicrous. But no matter how much I protest, my friends listen patiently to what I have to say as so much liberal claptrap, then repeat themselves, enumerating the weaponry, the drugs, the names of the gangs, *los 23, los popeyes, las mechas, las pirañas* (an all-girl gang), and so on. Children carry guns bigger than themselves. You can buy fragmentation grenades there for the equivalent of ten U.S. dollars. Nobody in their right mind would walk anywhere near there. And so it goes.

Who invited the paras? I ask a friend. She says most likely the police, who got the local businessmen to shovel out the money. Not a trace of cynicism or outrage in her voice. Our conversation shifts to an ex–M-19 *guerrillero,* who was assassinated by the paras recently. Rumor has it he was killed for supplying people in Carlos Alfredo Díaz with sophisticated weapons—*armas finas,* with an emphasis on the *finas.* For a while in the early 1980s, the M-19 guerrilla had a camp there with loudspeakers perched up high on rickety bamboo poles. He exuded mystery, this ex-*guerrillero;* strongly built, gentle in manner, with a clarity of vision that seemed only possible for someone who had, so to speak, left society for the wilderness of guerrilla warfare and then returned, blessed with the insights of exile. Given that, and his work on addiction among kids—which meant he mixed a lot with the gangs—I can see he'd make a target from the point of view of those (and they are many) who have not only given up on such kids but seem to take pleasure killing them, and found this man unfathomable. Being a *guerrillero* was bad. An ex-*guerrillero,* worse. But helping kids in gangs!

One of his cousins was mayor of the town for a few months before being removed by the opposition party on some sort of technicality they were able to dig up concerning a conflict of interest in the electoral campaign. But the real reason, according to the gossip, was that because of his connection with Carlos Alfredo Díaz, the mayor would not be tough enough on the youth gangs. Some went as far as to say he was an agent of the gangs. I find this incomprehensible, and relay it so you can get an idea of how monstrous these gangs of kids must seem. Not even the police can run them to ground. Hence there was something terrifying in this allegation, the image of a virtual gang member in charge of the town itself. Most telling, I think, is the story that people were against him because he was against the *limpieza.*

Variously known as "the barrio," or simply and most significantly as "the invasion," I keep wondering if the people who tell me about CAD in such vivid detail have ever been there. And what does it mean if all this imagery comes second- or third-

hand? The logic is cruel. Because the barrio is so dangerous, nobody dares go there, so people feed their fears through telling
one another these stories. But can it be entirely fantasy? There
must be some crucial connection with reality. But maybe that's
the inferiority complex of the ethnographer, not to mention
friend, who defers to the native's point of view? What I mean is
that you always submit to the authority of a trusted confidante,
that because she lives here all her life, and sees so many people
from different walks of life each day, she must get a true picture.
But maybe that's wrong? For surely a collective fantasy resists
truth and makes its own reality? I go round in circles, which only
gets more confusing when she tells me that either the police *or* the
guerrilla supply the barrio with arms.

Walking home I meet a lawyer in the street who used to work in
the municipal administration. Tells me things are only just beginning; that it is barely getting warm here. He is frightened. I can
see that. But he's also excited and trying to seem on top of things
with the tough-guy words he uses like "getting hot" and the deliberate understatement, "barely started." He wants to impress
me with the horror raging. Says the gangs are organizing an al-
liance for a counterattack on the paras or on the businessman
who brought them in. There could be a guerrilla attack on the
town any night now. Which is why the army is starting to patrol.
. . . If, as everyone says, the paras and the army are tightly
linked, I ask myself, why is the army patrolling here?

Could it be due to the threat of a guerrilla attack? It seems to
me unlikely, but then I think I underestimate both the actual dam-

age and the fear people have of being caught by cross fire between paras and guerrilla. They see themselves as of no account
to either side. I remember P. telling me how the shock of the first
guerrilla assault (the *toma,* meaning literally, "the taking of")
two years ago was likely to last years, buried in the town's collective memory. Nobody was physically hurt. The bank was blown
open around midnight with a bang that shook the sleeping town
to its marrow. People woke to find guerrilla soldiers on street corners telling them to stay in their homes. Within an hour the guerrilla had left and people poured into the town center to gape at the
ruins of the bank as kids fought for coins scattered in the gutter
and adults stole typewriters, computers, paper, whatever debris
from the bank they could get their hands on. It was a mob scene.
Other people like R. hid under the bed, just as they did during the
Violencia of the 1950s. The army turned up long after the guerrilla had left, leading people to say the army was incompetent or
scared. But there were rumors the roads were mined, and you
also had to consider that a confrontation between the army and
the guerrilla in town would be lethal for the townspeople.

When the guerrilla took the town the second time, one night
mid-2000, they blew open the safe in the bank, released prisoners
from the jail, and blew open most of the pawnshops, inviting
people to come and take what they wanted. Rumor has it they did
this because the pawnshop owners were not paying the *vacuna*
(protection money). Although it was at first said that the poor
were the pillagers, notably the people from CAD, it seems most
were from the better-off parts of town, some even arriving
in cars to carry off TVs, radios, pressure cookers, watches, and

the like. Several months later, some of these looters were mysteriously assassinated. I have heard that the pawnshop owners
were not only behind these assassinations but that they'd had a
big part to play in inviting the paras. But this is just a rumor. Like
everything else.

I was somewhat surprised by my friend's prediction that the
shock of the *toma*—the guerrilla "taking" of the town—would
remain for years. I thought people exposed to uncertainty and
danger for so long would be hardened, but then what does "hardened" mean? Perhaps people feared they would be caught in
cross fire between the army and the guerrilla? That's always in
the cards, but I think the trauma she's referring to is more the result of a diffuse foreboding of the guerrilla as a mysterious force
that erupts to give actual physical expression to the apocalyptic
fantasies that otherwise only hover around the edges of daily
awareness. A *toma* is very much a symbolic event in the theater
that is war, especially a war like this one, which is like no other.
As a performance involving exploding bank safes, kids fighting
for coins in the gutter at midnight, phantom guerrilla soldiers
swooping in at nightfall with who knows what in mind, a *toma* of
your town means you have become a chess piece in someone's
fantasy. That is not what you want to be.

I showed this diary to some undergraduate students at Columbia
University. We had been discussing how shock, as it occurs in
war, could be thought of as the result of trauma breaking
through a defensive shield built layer upon layer from exposure
to diffuse anxiety. One student, Amelia Moore, wrote that the

fears of a guerrilla counterattack—as I present those fears—are a release. "Shock has become a temptation in this diary," she concludes. "This secret desire for trauma, for a shock, is described on almost every page, though it is not explicated as such."[5]

Commenting on this desire for shock, Maria del Rosario Ferro writes me from Colombia: "As something is about to happen, people begin to announce events as a way to hold a certain kind of 'control,' and not let surprises overcome them. This in turn seeps through this diary of the ethnographer who is trying to digest all this information at that very moment. Or could it be that the whole logic of 'public secrets' is based on the desire of individuals to hold power over others by reproducing trauma, including the writer, who does not want to lose power over his readers? I do not believe this is a question of desire, though it might appear as such. I think it is more of a *limpieza*."

MAY 11

GIVEN THIS STATE OF AFFAIRS, is it any wonder that people take law into their own hands? A year before tales had begun to circulate of paras mysteriously at work in the region, death-lists were posted anonymously on the walls of the town. Most of those named were young men involved in gangs with a reputation for violent crime. The one posted on July 7, 1997, was signed by "The United Citizens." On top was a crude skull and crossbones with the word *DANGER* written underneath in English, and under that, in Spanish:

SI LA JUSTICIA NO LIMPIA EL PUEBLO
NOSOTROS LO HAREMOS

If the Justice System Does Not Clean Out the Town
We Will Do It Ourselves

There then followed a list of names with nicknames or aliases, as well as the names of the neighborhoods in which the person lived:

Castorina, the Indian from Carlos Alfredo Díaz
Alias Sánchez, assistant at the bus terminal
Ruben Mejía, brother of the black man "Perica" [name of a
  cocaine derivative] of Fifteenth Street
Alias Coche [automobile]—son of Tutu
Alias "the student"

Ominously, the list ended:

Y otros . . . [and others . . .]

I am told the lists are effective, at least in the short run. The aunts
of two people on the list told me their nephews split town even
though they had no money. Many people in the town support the
use of these lists; I'm not so sure they have much effect, but they
sure scare me.

The second list a week later had a quite different heading:

> *Instead of Trying to Defend the Lives of their Sons*
> *and Daughters that Appear in this List, their Parents should*
> *be disciplining them so They stop being Delinquents.*
> *Or Do They have the Right to Mug, Knife and even*
> *kill the Good People of this Town?*
>
> *What do you say Dr. Murillo?*

The first named on this list was that of the lawyer. Here is how
it was written:

Murillo   Lawyer of the Delinquents

And under him came the names of three elected members of the town board who, according to rumor, had made a fortune from bribes received for setting up the tax-free "industrial park." Then followed some thirty names, each one tagged as an alleged drug dealer, arms trafficker, or spy for a different gang.

Nobody I consult knows quite how to interpret this list—or the one that follows—but some people chuckle as they scratch their heads trying to figure who could have composed it. There is a lot that makes no sense, but there is satisfaction in having these public secrets "outed."

My thoughts go back to the journalist in Bogotá who told me that whenever she writes, she asks herself how Castaño is going to react. "But," she went on to say, "most journalists in Colombia are killed for exposing corruption."

Yet with these death lists—or rather the succession of death lists, with each subsequent one seeming to comment on the preceding one—it seems we have type of wall-poster journalism dedicated to the exposure of corruption. Here the anonymous author does not so much run the risk of being killed, as threaten to kill, a threat that triggers a firestorm of counterthreats.

The third list appeared three days later and was again different:

*Senor Mayor and Honest Citizens of the Community This is
the Frightening Truth and Secret behind These
Distinguished Citizens*

There followed the names of:

The commandant of the police, subtitled as "*comandante* of
the squadron of death" and as "smoker"

The businessman who owned the local lottery, described in
the list as "hired killer responsible for the assassinations carried out by the *comandante* of the police"

The town's notary, alias "the notary drug-dealer in marijuana
of '87, specializing in explosives, grenades, and a swindler"

Garrafa, butcher, buyer of stolen cattle together with . . .
[*Garrafa* is a nickname. It refers to a bulbous-shaped bottle of
aguardiente, resembling the shape of this man]

And so the list went on, naming the town's most respectable
not to mention richest citizens, ending with a footnote: *"These are
the true delinquents."*

Naming names is all-important, as in the death lists no less
than in my inability to name in this diary, as in the multiplicity
of names for the paras, no less than in the meticulous attention
to nicknames on the death lists. Nicknames inject a note of lev-
ity into the specter of death, alongside the implicit statement
that we are all in this together; we know one another's secrets;

we inhabit the one town, the one history, and the one system of justice.

A public meeting is called a week later on account of these death lists. The atmosphere is tense. The police are the main suspects. The majority of the thirty to forty people here are police, laden down with their uniforms, weapons, and heavy faces. The beady-eyed captain of police intelligence fixes me with bloodshot eyes. An overweight white guy in dirty black tennis shoes, he is the first to talk. He is the only who stands when talking. What does he want to tell us? That human rights are precisely what the police stand for; that human rights means respect for the law; and that the problem is that the young have no respect for authority, not even for their own family. (There are no young people at our meeting.)

The public defender from the provincial capital speaks next. "Colombia is a sick society," he says. "All its institutions are sick. As for the law, it keeps on changing. We are living in a crisis of institutions and we have to pull together. To say we are sick is not to be pessimistic. It's better to prevent than cure. Whenever there is a problem in Colombia, people reach for the latest version of the constitution. But what we have to do is study the social situation. There have always been death lists in Colombia. In the colonial period they put up names of conspirators so as to have them assassinated. During the *Violencia* this century, we had plenty of lists, as you can see in the film *Los condores no se entierran todos los días*. These lists are dangerous! Make no mistake! It is very important that police intelligence determine who is behind these lists—but to be successful, such intelligence has to have the collaboration of the town. People always say the police are behind the lists, but here," he adds, "the police have good relationships with the *delincuentes,* so I don't think that will happen."

The public defender speaks for almost forty minutes. He uses no notes. He asks how the young people on the lists are going to be brought into the discussion, and concludes by suggesting that all government officials should donate private time to prevent crime, and that Committees of Human Rights should be set up in all parts of town and out in the countryside. Human rights is not a monopoly of the left or of the guerrilla, he says. These committees should have representatives of the Church and of worker's unions. He pauses to tell us that such a committee established in a poor barrio in the state capital in 1991 had all its members except the president assassinated.

The captain of police intelligence stands up and takes our photo.

Two years later the public defender had to flee the country with his family because of death threats.

A young woman with a small child asleep on her lap introduces herself as a district attorney (*fiscal del circuito*). She points out that unemployment among the young is around 35 percent, that the huge paper factory has provided no jobs for local people, and she fears the same will happen with the new factories springing up daily. Hence there will be more crime. Every day she and her colleagues are presented with cases of people charged with possession of illegal arms. They ask them, "Why [do] you carry a weapon?" And they reply, "For security."

Another twenty police have just arrived to work here. At least that's what I hear. (How do people get to know these things? Why do they think they are true?) That would make a total of around 40 police, giving a ratio of 80 police per 100,000 population, compared with 196 per 100,000 for all of Colombia in the early 1990s, 257 in the U.S., 230 in Australia, 350 in Peru, 368 in Austria. But where are they in the midst of this slaughter? The town seems without police presence, except for a heavily sand-bagged "bunker" in the middle of the town, with all manner of obstacles on the road on either side of the bunker, itself sand-wiched in a row of homes in which people continue to live. Now and again you see police looking plenty scared dashing around in a pickup. You never ever see a group of cops stationary, and you never see a cop alone.

There had been two *retenes,* or police roadblocks, along the road that led to Cali ever since I first visited in 1969. The traffic had to stop and the police would cast a glance, maybe enter the bus or open up the car, maybe even ask for I.D.s. These *retenes* no longer exist, but now and again you see a mobile police detachment stopping cars—not buses—where the road hits the highway. What happened to the *retenes?* I ask a young friend who completed his military service three years ago. They make the police too vulnerable, he answers. *Catch-22.* If you don't have a sandbagged, concrete, or brick *reten,* you are vulnerable. If you have one, then even more so.

This strange but familiar logic is being repeated as I write these lines in the neighboring village, ten minutes south, close by the old slave hacienda surrounded by huge trees with an ancient cemetery to one side. The village is now the site of construction of two buildings that proudly signify its coming-of-age as a municipality: a small hospital and a police station. The first thing to notice is that these two buildings are situated in the center of the village so that an attack on the police would put civilians at extreme risk. The second thing to notice is that the hospital and the police station are smack up against each other. By using the sick as a barrier against the guerrilla, the police can once again show the world how the guerrilla have no respect for human rights, so a young friend living there tells me.

Then there's the size of the police station—three stories high, including the subterranean basement. It boasts thick walls like a medieval castle, built with "Arab technology," the locals tell me in awe as we muse over the growing shell of this fortress destined to take 60 cops for a village of maybe 3,000 people. A school had to be demolished to make room for it, and the village was so fiercely divided that police had to be called in. Half the people wanted the police station so as to provide security for the village, while the other half argued it made the village more likely to suffer a guerrilla attack. People who lived near the police station were vociferous in their opposition.

I was surprised to hear old friends of mine living there support the building of a police station. Two years ago they were telling me in no uncertain terms how afraid they were of police and how glad they were that none were stationed in the village, as police made crime worse. But now we are a municipality, they said, "the state has to have a presence."

Over the years I have seen peasant kids grow up and become po-
licemen. I often wonder how they turned out, these barefoot boys
taken far away to do their policing. Could they, too, have turned
into these horribly corrupt figures you keep hearing about—or,
worse still, don't hear about because people are too scared to
talk? E. shocked me when he retired from the force, came home
from Huila, where he had been stationed, and went back to work
on his dead father's farm, one of the few left in the neighbor-
hood. His own son had been knifed a month back for his tennis
shoes, but even though his assailants tried to kill him and he had
to be taken to the hospital, E. did not go to the police and make an
official charge. "It's a waste of time," he told me, "and you make
enemies. With the denunciation, the person you accuse wants revenge and [does] even worse to you . . . What's more, if you go
to the police, suddenly you find you're being held on suspicion of
something and have to pay to get out of it." He was scathing: the
jails are full of innocent people; the punishments are too light;
and the prosecutors are ineffectual on account of the volume of
work. They cannot see above the files of cases heaped on their
desks. If anyone knows, it's E., the ex-cop. His cynicism was
frightening. Was this the same shy E. I had known years ago gal-
loping bareback late afternoons on his father's chestnut colt? His
intensity scared me. Just the two of us face-to-face as the setting
sun set aglow the ruins of what had once been a powerful peasant
agriculture. There seemed no way out, and I hugged this bitter
image of him as I walked away along those muddy paths through
a war-torn landscape of ramshackle huts alongside holes like

bomb craters filled with water. As the peasant plots shrink to less than half an acre, peasants sell the remaining topsoil to the brick factories along the main road, owned by whites from Cali. This means they are selling their livelihood. Next they'll be selling their kidney, maybe an arm. The holes fill with water in which the kids love to swim among the water lilies.

The succession of death lists highlights the to-and-fro of what we could call "class warfare," reflected in the fact that it is not only the kids in the poor parts of town who are assassinated. The local businessmen go down, too. But I doubt they are killed by the poor. Take the case of Garrafa, the butcher. He is one of four brothers, white guys, grandsons of the *mayordomo* whom the landlords brought with them from eastern Colombia to clean out the uppity black peasants after the War of the Thousand Days at the beginning of the twentieth century, when power tilted to the Conservative Party. One brother inherited his father's position managing the estate and is still alive, perhaps because he wields little power since the estate was largely sold off to sugar interests. Another brother, however, became a key operator in the acquisition of peasant farms for the expanding sugar plantation owned by a Jewish emigrant family from the USSR. This brother was slick and smart. Very smooth. Good CEO material. You would see him accelerating his Nissan jeep through the peasant plots and across dusty roads out in the cane fields in those early days when cars were rare. He reeked of power, yet was assassinated a few years back, some say by the guerrilla, for his having screwed the peasantry. Others say he was killed by a professional—a *sicario*—paid by a woman peasant angry because he sold her land to the plantations with inaccurate boundaries.

The fourth brother was a labor contractor hiring gangs of black women and children for the plantations. He was found dead in his car, slumped over the steering wheel. His family put it about that he'd had a heart attack. Others say he was killed by a needle through the back of the neck. Seems like he was involved in criminal gangs, called *bandas,* that are different from the *pandillas* of the young. It is said that the night before this fourth brother was found dead, people living near the family farm a mile out of town couldn't sleep with all the commotion going on, what with trucks coming and going with strange cargoes. One of his friends, a butcher, told me the police killed him and that he was in fact head of a *banda* involved in stealing cattle and cars. People would come to the butcher to cash checks made out by this brother. His elder brother, the butcher, one of the two surviving, now slinks from corner to corner, a furtive shadow of his former bulbous self.

Rotund and beefy, the butchers stand in the marketplace sharpening their long knives, resting their elbows on their greasy white aprons. Early in the mornings before the sun rises they slosh around the town's low-lying brick slaughterhouse a few blocks from the central plaza, supervising the killing and butchering of the cattle and hogs they have bought for the day's market. A queue of poor people stand outside in the cold to drink the warm blood.

What gives with these butchers? When Juan Manuel was telling me about *limpiezas,* the first story he told me was of a butcher friend of his rounding up friends at night in the pickup and heading off with weapons into the drunken night. Butchers do not just sell meat.

They buy livestock from local haciendas and become friends with the landowners with upward of fifty acres and maybe a little coca laboratory hidden in a bamboo grove. Generally white or slightly colored, these landowners and the town's butchers together constitute a subculture that I think is pivotal in negotiating the see-sawing balance between business and crime, blacks and whites, country and city. Now and again these small-scale white landowners come into this proletarianized town full of diesel fuel and grease to show off their expensive little *paso fino* horses lifting their forelegs sharply clip-clop on the hard macadam, whooping it up in honor of the gods of a previous mode of production when expensive horses and cattle haciendas existed.

"These are the true delinquents," it had said on the third death list. How is it that while the *pandillas* or gangs of the young preoccupy everybody to the point of collective hysteria, the *bandas* of the local upper class rarely get talked about? Is it because the *bandas* have for so long been part of reality and that many people, or at least many influential people, get fat on them? It's as if the kids copied the norm but instead of keeping it secret gave it exposure. They gave it theater. They took it too far. But they got no money, just blood, glory, and eventually they got the paras.

You see that glory with their funerals. The young gangsters stand on the cemetery wall, profiled against the sky like the buzzards at the slaughterhouse, one next to the other. Never has anyone done that before. They carry the coffin through the streets from house to house of the gang members, arriving at the cemetery with a portable radio blasting rap. The clothes are dazzling. They carry guns. Anything could happen. Death itself has been refashioned like the clothes, the music, and the haircuts. This is the new Colombia.

First time I saw this was 1999. Another funeral was taking place at the same time. The crowds got mixed up for a moment. In the other funeral, women were crying and screaming by the grave, the men quietly standing in their worn suits with bowed heads. But with the young gangsters it was all defiance. Not grief. For them, death was violence and the violence was cause for protest, not acceptance. For them, death was the occasion for inventing tradition, not its reassertion.

People came from near and far. They came to ogle and be petrified. It is the scariest crowd of which I have ever been part, like an exposed nerve, muscles twitching, sensitive to the slightest change in temperature or breeze on the cheek.

Suddenly there is a mad churning, people screaming in pandemonium pouring out of the cemetery. What is it? What has happened? Someone says a person fell into the cemetery off the wall. Another says a gun was pulled. Still another says a fight has broken out. Others stare blankly. I push my way through the churning bodies into the entrance of the cemetery to see two young women in sizzling clothes fighting each other between the walled containers of the bones of the dead. One hits the other over the head with an empty paint can. The victim in fawn-colored overalls with huge silver buckles on the shoulder finds an empty brandy bottle and smashes its bottom off against the wall to make a weapon. They drift down a path between graves. I am told the dead person was killed by someone in his own gang.

The mourners in the other funeral stand by the open grave of an old woman from a peasant hamlet a few miles out of town. They know me and ask if I will take photographs of them with the corpse, which they insist on unveiling by lifting the lid of the coffin lined in shimmering white cloth to reveal a face made up with lots of rouge. She was only fifty when she died. Despite the poverty of the family, the coffin is ornate because death in this town is the occasion for displays of luxury. But the pit into which the coffin is going is the absolute definition of reality. It is deep. It is square. And the earth is a grubby gray, not the rich black color of the earth of the peasant farms that comes from millennia of volcanic ash floating down from the skies of prehistory. Immaculately straight, the sides of the grave display the marks of the shovel. The grave digger once told me how tricky his job is. He has to dig the grave just before the coffin arrives, before there is time for the bottom to fill with the foamy sewage water underlying the town.

The mourners of the gang walk to their grave in a straight line. Kids from twelve to twenty years old. Boys in Tommy Hilfiger shirts and square-sided haircuts, some with hair hanging over the shoulders. Baggy shorts. They are drinking *aguardiente* and playing the boom box as loud as they can. I am grabbed by someone from the woman's burial and cautiously steered through the flowing crowd to the exit lined by statuesque young women, wreaths of gold and white flowers at their feet, sucking on white ice-blocks sold from a pretty little cart with a parasol called *El Nevado,* "the Snowy Peak." The street in front of the cemetery, a block long, is packed with people ten-deep. The carts have their bells tinkling, joyous in comparison with the somber church bells we heard before.

Out of nowhere another mad panic breaks loose. People are running toward me as I talk with a friend from the countryside. I can't run, on account of a recent operation on my leg. People disappear down side streets. On the back of one of the gang member's shirts is written, in English, DEATH IS NATURE'S WAY OF SAYING SLOW DOWN.

Apart from death, you can slow things down by bunkering yourself deep behind brick, steel, and one-way mirrored glass. This last item—the glass—I discovered when I went to visit my friend L. in one of the poorer parts of this poor town. Her window against the street is a gift from her daughter, a single mother working as a servant in Caracas, Venezuela. Before this, L. had the most dungeon-like house on the block. And certainly no glass windows. In fact, when I first came to this town, late 1969, no houses had glass. Now with this dark glass, her house looks sinister and smart. Like all windows here, it is heavily barred. Another addition to the house is that the front door, solidly constructed sheet metal, has another door in front of it, a set of bars on a separate system of hinges. Most houses in the poorer parts of town now have this device.

She tells me that a victim of the paras has just been found out in a cane field, by sugarcane cutters, with rope burns around the neck and swollen testicles. Her nineteen-year-old daughter solemnly assures me 100 percent of the young people here have AIDS.

On the way home I stop at the herbalist's stall in the market-place, where a woman asks for plants to deal with an errant boyfriend. The herbalist is busy with other requests for plants and offers advice with confidence and humor derived from de-cades in the business. Hard to distinguish what is magical and what is not. Do I have to? Reaching into hidden recesses for a particular plant, his hands are a blur of motion while he maintains a steady patter of conversation. A great storyteller, he sells plants from all over southwest Colombia, a mountainous, verdant ter-rain of tropical rain forests and swampy mountain plateaus known as *páramos*. Each plant has a story, if you press him, for he is from the Putumayo, the upper Amazon, whose peripatetic In-dians are famous for their plant-lore and curing of physical ill-nesses and sorcery as well as just plain bad luck. A port in the storm, this is the sort of person we need, I say to myself, to deal with the paras.

Close to home I have a haircut at Amparo's, surrounded by a bevy of beauties having their toenails painted. Ten minutes. Best haircut ever; makes me look about fifteen, such a strange fifteen-year-old with gray hair and a serious face. In this brightly lit cap-sule of fantasy and hope dedicated to female beautification, life overflows, mirrored with possibilities of transformation. I am re-minded of the book fair in Bogotá.

In the street I meet Juana from Carlos Alfredo Díaz, who tells me it's true that the paras want to eradicate the entire barrio. Farther down the street, close to home, F., who loves to spin macabre tales, tells me CAD is more dangerous than ever. Nobody can go there. They'll strip you clean. Only two weeks ago a nurse in the clinic there was kidnapped by two men on a motorbike and found in Hacienda La Pampa with his tongue extruded, eyes gouged, and testicles twisted. Nobody knows by whom or for what.

When I get home, I find P., my host, tense, saying Ramón and I should be more careful not to go out on the street so much, especially by the town hall, where the politicians and their riffraff gather.

F.'s venerably aged mother sets off to the regional capital three to four hours away to pay taxes on her store and farm. Amid all this mayhem life goes on, an old lady boards a bus to go pay taxes! She seems more worried about the taxes than being stopped by guerrilla on the highway, notorious for such. A crotchety old dame with all the vim and vigor for which the *paisas*—people from the province of Antioquia—are famous, she loathes Andrés Pastrana, the president of the country, even more than she loathes the guerrilla, whom she detests. No doubt the president could learn a lot from her about how to negotiate a deal with Tirofijo, or "Sureshot," leader of the 18,000-strong FARC guerrilla who seems to have the president twisted around his little finger. Like F.'s mother, Tirofijo is a *paisa* from the north of the Cauca Valley and, like her, was a successful businessman and still is—only the nature of his business has changed. Even as an adolescent way back in the 1940s, it appears he was making good money from contracts with the local municipalities before the Conservative Party and their paramilitaries, the *pajaros* and the *chulavitas,* killed sections of his family belonging to the Liberal Party. But the president of Colombia knows little of this sort of suffering firsthand. Privileged son of a former president, with a future assured in the UN or similar transnational bureaucracies headquartered in Paris, New York, or Geneva, he appears to have no understanding of how most people live day to day and what makes them tick. (What president does?) F.'s mother is particularly incensed at his having conceded to the FARC a safe area the size of Switzerland in the forests of the Caquetá province bordering the Putumayo province in the south of Colombia. Like a lot of people I speak to, she wants the U.S. to invade and plaster the central mountains with napalm from beginning to end to eliminate the guerrilla! No doubt it would be a different country if she were in charge. One thing that impressed me about her was the ease with which she, a white woman, related to her black neighbors and to the townspeople in general. She tells me she has more than one hundred godchildren around here.

She also has relatives living in Atlanta about whom she is very proud. And thanks to a dating organization in Cali hooking up Colombian women with U.S. men, her daughter, F., has received telephone calls and letters in English, which she cannot speak or read. She shows me some of the letters, formulaic and insipid, and giggles as I translate. Fantasies of romance fly back and forth from north to south. Men also come in person to check out the women whose photographs and details they obtain through this agency. But it must take a lot of determination to travel to Colombia these days. Other women from here migrate to Italy as prostitutes. A woman three doors away brought an Italian husband back to the town—a most unusual event. Far older than she, he was horrified and soon left, alone.

I am bombarded with images of paramilitary killings. M. tells me that when the *pistoleros* (as he calls the paras) killed three prisoners just released from jail, the police apprehended them at the scene of the crime but then set them free. "They work together," he explains. Two women who allegedly sold drugs were killed one month back by a grenade hurled into their home. A young man drunk early evening in the center of town shouted out, *"¡Que salgan esas hijeputas!"* "Get the fuck outta here, you arseholes." He was shot down there and then, and nobody dared attend to his body, left lying in the street. Two youngsters were assassinated at ten in the morning in bright daylight in front of the church in the plaza, kids who had "problems with the law." Another youngster shot by the paras didn't die but was taken in an ambulance to Cali, stopped by guys on motorbikes, and killed inside the ambulance right there on the main road. A mad woman living one block from the plaza was assassinated because she was *una viciosa* (i.e., drug-addicted). And so it goes.

At sunset I visit friends who live at the end of the town in the street before Carlos Alfredo Díaz. Histrionic as ever, F. pleads with me as I prepare to leave. "Miguel! Don't go! Don't go!" she wails. Her brother was killed near that part of town (but that was at night in a pool hall). She is raving about *chuzos* (stabbings), *chuzos, chuzos, chuzos,* till the word rings in my ears as I walk down the streets she makes me fear.

When I get to my destination I see there is a metal-grill door in front of the usual sheet metal. Shuffling to greet me, R. thinks he's cured his prostate with tagua nuts from the Pacific coast. Last time I saw him he was walking with an inflated belly and a tube from his urethra into a bottle. Back in 1997 he was scared he was bewitched, his abdomen was so inflated. There is a magic from the Chocó province that uses toads and makes the victim's stomach rise and fall with the tides, or is it the moon? I forget. Not that sorcery is common here. Not on the surface, at least. His daughter, in her thirties, in a gorgeous blue silky blouse, with a small child sleeping in her arms, tells me she can't sleep at night—*muy atensionada*—on account of her fear of the front door being broken down and thieves entering, stealing the TV or worse. She is the only woman musician in a nine-piece band in Cali, but there hasn't been work in ages. Through the iron grill that secures the front entrance I watch the street outside get darker. The wall of the house opposite goes gray, then fades into blackness. A woman walks by quickly and quietly. In a soft voice as silken as her blouse, the daughter tells me we cannot talk about the *limpieza*.

White lace curtains divide the living room where we are sitting from the bedroom. B. died ten years back from emphysema and *nervios*. All their life she and R. washed and ironed clothes for a living day and night in this same room, seven days a week, and for most of that time the iron was heated by a smelly gasoline flame. In those days this town was full of men from the jungles of the Pacific coast cutting and loading sugarcane who had neither time nor the skills to wash or iron their clothes, so R. and B. found a livelihood washing for them. She smoked an awful lot, too; was so skinny at the end, a twisted knot of tendons and arteries with blue veins coursing between, her hair in a tight bun. Three years back their son died, hit on his bicycle by a car. Traffic accidents seem to kill as many people in Colombia as do bullets.

Gray stuffed plastic furniture, sweet little coffee cup on a large clear glass plate brought especially for me. The youngest son is a talented pianist, but there's no piano here. Like many people in this town he has abandoned the Catholic Church and has become a fundamentalist Protestant, in his case a Baptist, and sings negro spirituals from the U.S. in English with a small choir. He now works as a psychologist, a great advance for such a poor family, and has a part-time job paid for by the municipal administration. His group at work has focused on the question that interests me more than any other: Why are the kids today so violent? (I must sound like an old fogey.) Yes! he says. Kids born since the 1980s are twisted because of three reasons: (1) The *Violencia* of the 1950s; (2) unstable families; and . . . we never got to the third reason.

Why am I so disappointed? It seems like people's street-smart wisdom evaporates when translated into these professional categories of thought. I am reminded of a seminar on violence to which I was invited by researchers in the school of public health at the University of Cali two years before, where I had the same feeling, even worse. They would station investigators in emergency rooms of hospitals and fill out questionnaires that would be quantified on computers in accord with epidemiological models imported from the Harvard School of Public Health, which supplied them with their grants, violence being seen largely as a medical—not a political—problem, best analyzed by statistics. At the seminar on violence I attended, the investigators did their show-and-tell thing: how many people of what sex of what age had died or been violated by what sort of weapon between what hours on what night of the week . . . It became painfully obvious that so busy were they perfecting their methods of measurement that they had lost sight of what the measurements were for. In losing sight of the soul of violence, they had lost their own souls to it. And they are not alone. Most books on violence published in Colombia—and there are many, although I have not counted them—are statistical encounters with death and consist largely of squabbles with other people's measurements, which should, you would think, suggest that perhaps violence cannot be measured. Capping it all is an influential publication from the nation's top university, La Universidad de los Andes, entitled *Crime and Impunity*, subtitled *Precisions on Violence*, and, just in case you didn't get the point, concluding with the chapter "Measure, Measure, and Measure Some More."

Dostoevesky's *Crime and Punishment* provides an alternative way of thinking about crime to *Crime and Impunity*. He takes us into the human soul where religious forces and the city converge in a love of cruelty and the need for confession where the mind talks to itself. Obsession with measurement obliterates even the glimmers of such a necessary understanding of the desire to transgress the law. "You alone have understood me," was Dostoevsky's response to Strakhov, who had written: "This is not mockery of the younger generation, neither a reproach nor an accusation—it is a lament over it."

ASSASSINATION STATISTICS. A friend knows somebody who works as a clerk in the Civil Registry office. Two years ago I went there looking for figures on homicide, and I was blown off. I went everywhere trying to get the numbers—the Attorney General's office, the hospital, and finally the CTI, the new corps of police meant to be trained in modern, scientific methods of crime detection. Wherever I went, I was directed somewhere else or given "incomplete" figures. At times it seemed like the figures were a state secret. If only I'd recorded that runaround in detail, it would have pretty well told you everything about Colombia, not to mention the magic of statistics. The truth is, nobody knows how many killings there are.

This time the homicide rates I get from the Registry in town, covering the period from January 2001 to April 2001, indicate 420 homicides per 100,000 population! Compare that with the U. S.'s of around 8, and Australia's rate of 1.8. Even the town of Florencia, capital of the Caquetá, generally considered the most violent place in Colombia, had a mere 207. And if we look to the recent past, we see a similarly dramatic fact. In 1998, what I got from the CTI police (inside contact, special favor) was a rate of 105 homicides per 100,000 in 1997, and 96 per 100,000 in 1998, a quarter of what's been happening in this town this year.

And what a shock to compare these figures with those for the dreaded *Violencia* of 1948–1958. The homicide rate for Colombia as a whole in 1948 was 16 per 100,000. It doubled the following year to 30 and peaked at 51 per 100,000 in 1958.[6] Back in the bad old days, a murder rate of 51 was off the charts.

In the end, the numbers numb, burning themselves up as soon as they appear in the dark firmament of our ignorance. They evade our grasp, eager to control reality through quantifying it. Worse still, numbers drain the meaning out of the stuff being numbered. How do you imagine the difference between 420 and 207 homicides per 100,000? What can that possibly mean? How do you understand the intricacies of situation and human motive filtered through mean streets and meaner histories? Moreover, the accuracy intrinsic to numbers is wholly belied in the case of Colombia's death and violence by the devious, bloody, and rumor-riddled society that brings those numbers into being. How could you possibly expect honest statistics in a war zone? Like corruption, numbers feed off truth. But unlike corruption, numbers flatten our understanding of the social world and the imagination that sustains it.

MAY 12

SATURDAY. IT'S TRUE. We don't go out after eight. Last night we sat down by the TV to watch the Miss Universe competition for which everyone here was waiting. It had barely commenced when in came a friend with a quiet but watchful partner who is introduced as a *compañero*, an agronomist from the Alto Naya, where the massacre occurred three weeks ago on the heights of the western *cordillera* running along the other side of the valley. With his arms tied behind his back he was forced at gunpoint to guide the paramilitaries for two hours to the peasant villages they wanted to massacre.

Meanwhile, Miss Universe plays on and our little group divides its attention between this man's tale and the TV. ("How like Colombia!" someone tells me later. "How like 'How Like Colombia,'" I feel like replying.) I ask the volume to be dropped as his words get lost in the interviews with the queens with their perfect smiles. They are asked if they had their lives over again, what would they choose to change? All except one say they would change nothing. "We're not going to waste ammunition on this scum!" is what the paras said, unsheathing their machetes. Two members of the guerrilla had passed over to the paras, so he said. It was they who pointed out the peasant "collaborators."

The paras proceeded down the slopes of the *cordillera* toward the sea. There are no roads, maybe a path here and there. As soon as the river is deep enough, people resort to dugout canoes. From hamlet to hamlet the paras proceeded, killing their way, but lost their nerve as the guerrilla began to pursue them. It seems that the paras do not do well in forests or away from Colombian army support. Some drowned, and the remainder sought refuge with the Colombian navy stationed at the mouth of the River Naya at Puerto Merizalde. In this way these have been, to my knowledge, the first paras ever to have been "captured" by the armed forces of the Colombian government. Has that had any effect? A friend writes me in early June, two months later, that people are still fleeing the Naya area and that some have traveled as far south as the Timbiquí River on the Pacific coast. She also informs me that the original estimate of scores of peasants killed has been scaled back to eighteen.

Some sixty people were reported dead at that time—but we will never know how many—with the usual horror stories. Many people fled east back into the Cauca valley just south of Cali to find refuge in small towns such as Timba and Santander de Quilichao, towns taken over by the paras the past two years. Out of the frying pan and into the fire. The paras mount roadblocks, check the I.D.s of everyone passing, and limit the food and med-. icine anyone can take through, in case it's for the guerrilla.

Coca has been cultivated and prepared in the Naya region

since at least ten years ago when my anthropologist friend first worked there. She was pregnant. "How's the Nayera?" the peasant-colonists would ask, endowing the unborn child with honorary citizenship of what, today, is no longer their home but a name carried in memory of fond encounters long ago in the mountains. Now my friend has gotten a job in a government-funded project to assist people fleeing the massacre.

She told me of a man who used to walk to the Alto Naya hours and hours on a mountain path to sell ice-blocks made in the valley. He would then return home to Corinto, on the other side of the valley, with his Styrofoam box full of coca. The guerrilla had a good thing going there, and that is why the paras moved in. Where there's wealth, sooner or later a chain reaction occurs. You have to know about this if you want to understand what's happening to Colombia. This is basic.

First is the *vacuna*, meaning vaccination—you pay a little to the guerrilla and you don't get a fatal, contagious disease and everyone is happy; the cows stay put, the family stays whole, and everyone smiles at the clever little joke of the *vacuna*. In areas of colonization like the Alto Naya, the guerrilla will establish their own state, with strictly enforced laws prohibiting adultery and drug taking, regulating alcohol as well as protecting the environment. And then come the paras, especially if there are drugs.

Setting up a state within the state in Colombia by guerrilla groups goes back a long way, at least to the days of the infamous *Violencia* beginning in the late 1940s when the state was hijacked by the Conservative Party, which, with the aid of the paramilitaries of the time, massacred peasants of the left-leaning Liberal Party, forcing them to form self-defense groups and guerrilla bands. What is perhaps surprising is the alacrity with which legal codes were created by these groups. The 1953 guerrilla Law of the Llanos (the eastern plains) details 224 articles, including control of prices. In the guerrilla Law of Southern Tolima of 1957, one finds articles covering use of firearms, consumption of alcohol, restrictions on travel (which requires a passport), pasturage of animals, public disturbances, and conformity to an already established "family code." Punishments take the form of fines and free labor. There is no imprisonment, and capital punishment is strictly ruled out except in the case of treason. As for the motive behind the code? That is simple. The very first words of the Law of Llanos explain it: the government's administration of justice is inept.[7]

The language and style of thought of these codes is impeccably statist and bureaucratic, suggesting that the body of Colombian law served as the template, changes being made where ideology or the exigencies of guerrilla war demand it. But what writers call "the voice" remains the same; this distant, forceful voice of authority which, with every breath, translates force of arms into the force of reason. In other words, a legal mentality is by no means foreign to the Colombian tradition of guerrilla warfare, and the "state within a state" concept of political philosophy is well entrenched. What stands out, in fact, is precisely the dense interweaving of arms and law. Is it surprising, therefore, that the deadly enemies of the guerrilla, namely the paramilitaries of the late twentieth century, would imitate them, trying to set up their own little republics within the republic, as is happening in this town?

My anthropologist friend ends many of her stories with "the sandwich." Everybody sooner or later gets to be in the sandwich, meaning that ever-diminishing space between the guerrilla and the paras. If you're seen as having supported the other side, even under threat, then you're to be killed. Next day, close to the central plaza in my town, I see a new restaurant named El Palacio del Sandwich.

I ask her if, because of her work, she's afraid of being *amenazada?* I wonder if it sounds as bad in English? *Amenazada* means "threatened." It's not the language that is the problem. It's a matter of understanding a practice: anonymous phone calls, maybe a letter or your name on a photocopied list stuck to a wall. It could come from relatives fighting over property, could be the local rotary club–hacienda-cattlemen types, could be an organized death squad, guerrilla, who knows. But it is enough to get most people packing. Except her. She laughs. "In Colombia we are all *amenazada,*" she says.

The young man who was forced to act as a guide for the paras was born close to the Alto Naya and he tells us the FARC guerrilla has been there for more than ten years. Nearly all the guerrilla fighters are Indians from the mountains running north to south along the other side of the valley, the eastern side. Yet black colonists have been making farms up in the Alto Naya for at least twenty years. It is said by my black friends in the south of the Cauca valley and on the Pacific coast of Cauca that there are

few black people among the guerrilla, at least in southwestern
Colombia (where there are huge black populations), and that the
majority of the guerrilla in this conflicted part of Colombia are
Indians from the mountains of the *cordillera Central*. Even in the
FARC camp at Saija, deep in the humid rain forest of the sweltering Pacific coast, which also has an overwhelming majority of
black people, there are only four blacks, a friend who visited
there not so long ago, delivering an outboard motor, told me,
deeply appreciative of the beauty of the Guambiana Indian girl
warriors all the way from the mountains of the interior. My
young black friends in the south of the valley chuckle as they tell
me blacks are too wily to join the guerrilla. Only dummies who
take to discipline would join up. The stereotype held of black
municipal administration and other black organizations in this
area, held by blacks, whites, and Indians alike, is that the blacks
rarely form stable organizations. Yet many, perhaps a majority,
of the paras are from the Atlantic coast, the north of Colombia,
and there are many blacks from the Chocó among *them*.

I have never been to the western side of the valley since the paras
took it over just south of Cali, and I have little firsthand knowledge of the Alto Naya, where the massacre occurred in the
mountains three weeks back in April 2001. But I did visit a zone
with a similar history in the north of the valley, around the town
of Buga. I was invited by a schoolteacher who worked there
many years and knew the peasants in the mountains in that region. He showed me the army barracks by the barrier across the
only road leading from Buga to the mountains of the *cordillera*

Central. There's no way the army wouldn't know the paras went by on their way to cut people to pieces. "It was a terrible thing to see that apparatus," a young peasant man said in the newspaper, referring to the laptop computer the paras use when they pull into a mountain village to check their death list more than likely provided by army intelligence. Everyone evacuated the area immediately and came down the mountain to stay in Buga. I interviewed a few of the several hundred living in an enclosed basketball stadium. They had been there exactly a year, sad and scared to go home, their farms and animals gone. Even cornered in the stadium they were receiving death threats. Where else can they go? They cannot go back to their farms. The army says it cannot guarantee their security. What the army means, I think, is "We will kill you . . . either directly or by setting loose the paras." I was told by these peasant refugees that the army had supplied the paras with transport and even, on one occasion, helicopter gunship support when they engaged with the guerrilla that has been in the high mountains there for many years.

My contact in Buga told me a year later that there had been three successful attempts by the government to find new farmland for the refugees, yet each time the plan has failed due to opposition by peasants living close to the designated areas. They were either frightened that the refugees would attract paras in pursuit, or else they themselves accused the refugees of being *subversivos.*

In tiny writing, using printed letters, the schoolteacher kept a meticulous diary in a school exercise book with lined pages. In dispassionate language, similar to government bulletins, he tracked media reports on the paras and contrasted that with what peasants told him about the same events. It was a strangely bureaucratic document, but one bursting with irony, an appeal to time-honored traditions of enlightenment and truth as predestined to emerge in the light of day, one day, by means of a dossier like this one. But this diary suffered from strange lapses and jumps in time as if the task of writing these blocklike letters, like little soldiers marching across the page, had become too burdensome as events outstripped the scribe's ability to keep up.

The first entry was:

Antecedents

By means of graffiti and flyers, especially in Cali, there have been warnings of the forthcoming arrival in the Valley of the paramilitaries. There have also been notices in the newspapers with commentaries as to their possible presence (*El Pais*, 27 July and 30 July, 1999).

Arrival: 31-VII-99

The entry of the paramilitaries into the Valley was announced by a military action in the hamlet of La Moralia in the municipality of Tuluá (*zona media*) the 31st of July of 1999 in the hours of night. The community was celebrating the *fiesta* of its patronal saint so there were many people from there and from the surrounding hamlets. The paramilitaries, identified as *Autodefensas Unidas de Colombia* or AUC, *Bloque Calima*, or BC, arrived in three trucks with more than one hundred combatants along the road from La

Marina, which means that they would have had to pass the police post there or assemble close to that post in a hacienda or finca. . . .

[On August 2, after destruction of peasant homes and assassinations in the mountains between Tuluá and Buga] the TV news and the press show pictures of the AUC presence in the valley, but no local or regional authority admits to their existence.

There followed the registration numbers of the trucks and a lot of detective work ascertaining the identity of their owners. Page followed page. I wondered how many more of these secret diaries were being kept in Colombia.

*   *   *

Under a mango tree last night by the roadside, my bullfighter friend set up giant speakers, and about ten of us, blacks and whites, sat in a circle, drank *aguardiente*, and danced. It was an act of defiance even though it was not an area you would expect much attention from the paras. Occasionally a motorbike would cruise past, and I was surprised there was not more anxiety in our little group. P. had pleaded with me and Ramón not to go. Finally she broke down in anger and tears. She was furious. I thought for a moment she might even hit me. "Go then! And come back whenever you want! *¡Es asunto suyo! Pueden regresar a la hora que quieran. Mañana . . . Pero prevenir es siempre mejor.*" There was a dance hall around the corner from which people would emerge and look at us. A big white guy just stood there watching without moving, making me nervous. I wonder where I could dive for cover once the *balacera*, the shooting, starts. The people around me pretend not to see or be worried by him. At least I think they're pretending.

Thin as a wisp of smoke, standing stock-still in front of each seated person, the sister of a friend of mine pours out shots of *aguardiente*, moving slowly inside the circle under the open sky, flaunting her vulnerability. "I feel like a fly in milk," she tells me. In her white dress, her white face is expressionless, like a knife, still and thin, fragile as exposed bone in a wound. She has a quadriplegic nineteen-year-old son at home. "My baby," she says. None of her family help, she says. She has two daughters as well, ages ten and fourteen. Her face is a mask of pain, of steel like the sturdy grills people now put in front of their front doors. The greatest fear, the one you go to sleep with, if you can sleep, is of having your front door broken down by thieves or paras. I keep asking how she makes do economically and I get a weird feeling something is not right here, that she's a little too crazy, a little too hurt, and I have an awful sensation she's prostituting herself or her daughters, or both. How middle-class I am. It sweeps through my mind to be dispelled. The paralyzed son *"es la cosa más divina en mi vida, "* she says, "the most divine thing in my life."

Her husband was shot dead five years ago. A mechanic, he had gotten into drug dealing and failed to pay for an advance on fifteen kilos of cocaine. He gave a lot of it away to friends. Drank crates of whisky, holidays in San Andrés in the Caribbean, and ended up assassinated three blocks from home. A year later their kid, Miguel, dove into the river that runs through town, hit his head, and became quadriplegic. Someone told me he had been shot in the neck.

At the age of fourteen, Miguel stole a revolver from his uncle and joined the first gang to be created in this town. It was called Las Mechas, on account of the flowing long hair of its members. All gangs must have a name, I guess, all gangs other than the paras, who have a surfeit of names but none of them evocative. Las Mechas were led by the notorious Nemecio and were formed around 1992. It was huge gang and a huge novelty, the only game in town, rapidly attaining the status of a quasi-religious cult. But by 1997, I was hearing of forty-seven gangs (some people said there were only ten). When Nemecio was killed, by a nephew, I believe, his followers went wild, stampeding through the town in anger and pain. As he was dying they screamed at the nurses and doctors in the emergency room, "If you don't resuscitate him, you're dead! We'll kill you, too!" They carried the corpse around town in an open coffin to the homes of the gang members (not that so many have homes), and after he was buried a story started to circulate that his bones had been secretly dug up from the cemetery and taken to barrio Carlos Alfredo Díaz. There they were *arreglada,* or "fixed"—meaning subject to witchcraft—so they became magical and empowering, just like the Church does with the bones of its saints.

"Nemecio's house was full of porcelain," the quadriplegic boy's uncle later told me. He had gone to visit Nemecio to inquire about his revolver and his missing nephew. "What is porcelain?" I asked. "Ceramic panthers, tigers . . . that sort of stuff."

On hearing this, our taxi driver turned around and expressed an ardent desire for a porcelain panther, too. Later the uncle learned that, all the time there, with Nemecio and the porcelain panthers, his nephew was hidden in the rafters looking down on them as they talked with the revolver cocked.

It's midnight. Ramón and I want to leave the party. Just a few blocks home. No! They insist. You can't walk. We have to call a taxi. But there are no taxis after eight o'clock. P. told me the drivers are too scared, and there's no business, anyway. But they call some guy in a beat-up car, and he drives us those few blocks. A small country town under the stars in Colombia. Don't walk at midnight! Five days later the paras assassinated two people at that same corner at which we danced.

In the morning I ask a good friend about this strange mother. We glide into her dark bedroom, bed made with its white cover stretched tight. She opens the closet door to put clothes away and says she can't really say anything, it's too difficult. There is a barrier we cannot, dare not, must not cross. But I will. I must. I have to.

So hard to believe the violence here. It looks so normal most of the time. All the violence appears by means of stories or in the statistics I get from my friend's friend in the Civil Registry. I remember talking with a young Cali anthropologist, Gildardo Vanegas, who spent most of two years visiting Agua Blanca and Siloe, the two toughest slums in Cali. Many stories of murder came his way, but he told me he never witnessed overt violence.

Yet on the TV news every night, Colombia was drowning in blood. Which image was true? he asked me. This adds meaning to the title of his book published in 1998: *Cali: Behind the Masked Face of the Violences*. Near to where I live, an old lady regularly watches the early evening news and occasionally calls me in to watch, too. Ten minutes of horror pass before our eyes in which the guerrilla is blamed for just about everything and the army is always victorious. She maintains a rapid commentary of defiance and despair. Sometimes it seems she's a walking TV news herself, she's in such perfect harmony with the terror that is the media. What then of my two weeks' diary? What mix of truth and fantasy does it mediate?

I keep asking myself, What am I doing here? Adrift on an unspecified mission, something pulls me, but it will only be obvious when I arrive. If I arrive. Genet called his memoir *Prisoner of Love*, and as you read his sprawling book you get the idea that he, too, was aimless. His sense of fair play made it hard for him to support the leadership of the PLO. Professionally, so to speak, he insisted in preserving a critical distance, as any writer should, although he is by no means a neutral observer. His objectivity is partisan:

> I was always on the other side of a boundary. I knew I was safe, not because of a Celtic physique or a layer of goose fat, but because of an even shinier and stronger armor: I didn't belong to, never really identified with, their nation or their

movement. My heart was in it; my body was in it; my spirit was in it. Everything was in it at one time or another; but never my total belief, never the whole of myself.[8]

But he was in some sappy way in love, as his title says, and he was made captive by that. What exactly he was in love with is hard to say.

Add to that his sense, which I too feel, of rarely being able to communicate between two worlds: intellectuals and the poor; Colombia and the U.S.; city people and peasants—so many of these "two worlds"—such that mostly everything you write is fractured and incomplete searching for the in-between world, which, in the diary world, is that figment called yourself. This is another sort of imprisonment, not by love, so much, as by the impossibility of communicating experience. One thing seems increasingly certain to me and that is my respect for the autonomy of the intellectual world, side by side with an increasing love and respect for the things of the world, the nature of flowers, the peasant *fincas*, the body. . . .

I wonder what's it like to be talking of killings day in and day out for so many years? What does it do to you, to your understanding of the things of the world?

MAY 13

Sunday, Mother's Day; Día de la madre: worst day of my life. But first there was a visit from the ever-serious J., tall, bald, and bespectacled with his beautiful sonorous voice telling me that people are fleeing the barrio Carlos Alfredo Díaz for fear of attack by the paras, whom he refers to as *pistoleros*. (But let us not forget fear of attacks by gangs there, also.) More than forty houses have been abandoned, he says, and most everything has been stolen from them, including doors and windows. But it's not only from Carlos Alfredo Díaz that people are fleeing. They are escaping from all over town. Many go to a sugarcane town similar to this one ten miles away. But how long before the *limpieza* reaches there too?

Young and earnest, J. is trying to "raise consciousness," as he puts it, among the residents in CAD, and he does this with a small group of like-minded young people who meet once a week on its outskirts, in the second story of a house on the road leading out of town along which eighteen-wheeler trucks roar so often and loud it's impossible to hear anyone speaking. Instead, we look down onto the spectacle of CAD spread out below us on the other side of the tracks cutting through town. One of the things the gangs do, I'm told, is hold up these eighteen-wheelers at night on this road. I'm sure I'd be inclined that way, too, if I lived here, trucks belching past your home every minute of the day and into the night carrying untold wealth while you sit in misery.

Midmorning we go to visit the quadriplegic boy, Miguel. We cross a pedestrian bridge, eyeing the river below into which Miguel is said to have dived and broken his neck four years ago. There is little water running, and it is empty of people. Nobody swims in the river now. Years ago, kids dived off this bridge, and hundreds of women were scattered every day along the river-bank washing sheets and clothes. The cleansing rites by the river constituted part of the soul of this town, its unofficial law-court, source of news, confessional, and women's political forum. The river served that purpose since the first ex-slaves settled here. Paddle steamers from Cali made their way here regularly into the 1930s, but now the river has been drained of most of its water to irrigate the sugar plantations and what water remains stinks, contaminated by the paper factory that converts the squeezed sugar cane stalks known as *bagaₒo* into paper.

The uncle takes us through a barrio where he says there was a lot of drug dealing. We go around the corner, which he tells us is where they killed his brother-in-law, the paralyzed boy's father. We stop at the worst house in the unpaved street, like a garage with two barely functioning doors. The uncle peers through a

crack between the bricks, then knocks. A young white girl, age about ten, opens the door. Looks like she's been crying. She lets us in to a large empty space with a black woman sprawled diagonally over a bare mattress, two small kids whimpering by her side. It is midday and hot. There is a small bookcase against the wall with three red encyclopedias in it and a mirror above with a tray for makeup. The rest of the room is empty. But at the far end is a dark alcove with two beds close together. The bed against the wall is shrouded by a mosquito net suspended by broken broom sticks tied to the corners of the bed. In the bed is a head, a shrunken head with glaring eyes—the head of a boy, his entire body shrunken, and the arms bent tight at the elbows and at the wrists so that his hands festoon his chin. A large lump under the covers suggests his legs are contracted in the same way. His limbs are contracting into his head, and his head is contracting into his eyes. This is Miguel. There is a thick tube for urine leading into a jug on the concrete floor, and a TV up high near the ceiling showing a car race in England, then football and dancing cheerleaders, their mighty thighs marching across the screen.

He has been left in this bed, in the dark, for four years, more or less. His limbs have telescoped into his torso. I cannot believe this. I sit down on the other bed and ask him a couple of questions regarding the use of his arms, as if I am back to being a medical doctor. He tells me to shut the fuck up. The uncle, Ramón, and I sit in silence, the four of us watching the stupid TV for ten minutes. I ask, where can I leave the present for his mum? "Leave it with Miguel," says the uncle, so I leave it in its blue-and-white-striped plastic shopping bag on the bed.

The uncle says nobody visits the boy. His friends have either been killed in gang violence or have fled. The boy is so mean-tempered, snapping at everyone, says the uncle, that now he never visits either. He thinks the boy is being left to die. This is what happens in Colombia, he tells me, as if I am new here.

Months ago they called in a relative who is a doctor who said the boy's heart is failing. He faints if someone sits him up. He has no wheelchair. It is impossible to believe that the family on the mother's side or the father's side can't help. What has happened these past few years for people to give up and let the kid rot like this?

Later I speak with a doctor in Cali and arrange a consultation. The uncle thinks the boy will reject it. But he doesn't. He plans to practice being sat up so he can make the journey into Cali. The doctor is worried about raising false hopes. There is no coverage for long-term care, and a motorized wheelchair is impossibly expensive. Sometimes, rarely, when the surgical team from Los Angeles comes for its twice-yearly visit, you can get one. This is how things are in Colombia. And this is the same doctor who tells me he cannot say anything political in the hospital or clinic, because the paras are supported by the doctors' association. Two weeks later I find out the boy has decided not to go, and the mother is indifferent. His uncle was right.

We go home and cook a Mother's Day lunch for P. She has no children, but to me she is both mother and friend. N. has brought a bottle of red wine from Cali, where he goes weekly to call his family in Bogotá. We have no wineglasses, so we drink out of tiny shot glasses, wine being rarely drunk in these parts. The par-

alyzed boy's uncle is there. We are seven altogether. My friend the ex-inspector drops in, too. We have a grand time, then I pack a bag and leave. A week here is the outer limit for safety.

Late afternoon finds me back in Cali for the night in the "gated community" of my anthropologist friend. She is not home yet. Ramón and I sit waiting for her by the tiny swimming pool surrounded by palms. We are alone. Every so often an armed guard in a brown uniform walks by, ostentatiously casual. A sign says No Swimming Today. A sandal floats upside down in the pool. The breeze is soft. It comes every afternoon year-round in Cali, like a good friend, but it never reaches the low-lying sugarcane towns to the south and east where the air stays still. Being here is an escape, an escape from hell, from the immediacy of fear, into a pretense of normality that allows us to look back and reflect on the week we have just passed. We watch the reflection of the palms in the water as darkness gathers like a fist. The stillness of the reflection absorbs everything. Stilled of the necessity to talk, my body enters the image in the water and loses itself there, tears flowing into its flat, dead stillness.

THE SECOND WEEK

MAY 21

"BAD NEWS," P. tells me when I return after a week on the Pacific coast. "They're killing more and more have arrived. Last Friday, Eder Leandro was assassinated one block from where you were dancing under the mango tree. He was killed together with one other person in broad daylight. On the following Sunday two more young men were gunned down. One was shot leaving a store and managed to get to his home but they cornered him in the kitchen. Then they marched into another home but the young man they were hunting managed to hide in a cupboard and escaped." I try to imagine what it must be like to be trapped in the corner of your mother's kitchen with her beaten-up pots and pans you know so well as they open fire. The highland girl sits calmly at the sewing machine receiving a lesson from P. as we talk, just the three of us, as Ramón has continued his travels elsewhere. Nothing seems to phase her as she guides the material under the plunging needle.

"Was he a *delincuente*?" I ask P. "I don't know," she replies. "He has a brother who gets into trouble. . . ." I run into A. on his push-bike. He works as a morgue assistant for the CTI police and assures me, with the confidence of those who work with corpses, that all four assassinated were *delincuentes.*

Yet how can he be so definite? Not only do the paras kill persons who have no connection with delinquency, but there often seems no clear division between the criminal underworld and the law-abiding world resting upon it. The distinction is a necessary fiction. In reality what exists is a ragged continuum. Who decides where the continuum is to be divided?

Aren't the paras just another gang, indeed, the most violent one in town, whose code—if we may call it that—has merged with the code of "law and order"? Their position is no less ambiguous than their victims. Yet their law insists there can be no ambiguity. Only right—or wrong.

That afternoon I join a funeral procession for an assassinated *delincuente.* Two beat-up white cars lead the mourners, belching exhaust into their faces. I meet the tailor in the procession. He shrugs and raises his eyebrows. He must be sorry for the death—otherwise he wouldn't be in the procession—but he accepts it as the price for security. In the crowd milling about the cemetery gate, together with ice cream vendors ringing their bells, I run into L. and her sister E., whom I haven't seen in years. Hand conspiratorially over her mouth, L. whispers we musn't talk about the assassinations here in the street. But loud-mouthed E. claps me on the back and asks me belligerently for my opinion of the state of the country. The cocaine is organized by the rich, she says, who then blame the poor, who have no alternative but to get into trafficking.

In the early evening I talk with a lawyer born in the town. He tells me the so-called *pistoleros* are in fact the *autodefensas*—i.e., the name derived from the *Autodefensas Unidas de Colombia*, aka the AUC. The world of instituted violence is entitled by an alphabet soup of acronyms:

FARC (guerrilla)
ELN (guerrilla)
EPL (guerrilla)
AUC (paras)
FFAA (army of the state; doubling the letters provides an
    extra-strong dose of officialdom)

Not much poetry here. All these acronyms mimicking one another, each with the same exchangeable uniforms, weapons, and—who knows—pretty much the same mentalities, too? At least the youth gangs have a lyrical touch: *los popeyes, las pirañas,* and so forth.

It's not true that the *autodefensas* were invited by the local businessmen, the lawyer tells me. They invited themselves! But why come here, I ask, if their aim is to counter the guerrilla, yet there is no guerrilla presence here, at least no obvious one. He says the paras already exert a military presence in an arc of territory west of here and want to extend the area from the western chain of the Andes to the central chain and thus control this town in the center of the valley between the two mountain chains. They are not just after Communists or the guerrilla, nor will they kill only delinquents. They could easily turn on leaders and influential people here whom they see as obstructing their plans. Nevertheless, it is the kids running around with homemade shotguns and grenades that galvanize this paramilitarization. The lawyer is adamant. The gangs are the clear and present danger. Everyone in town agrees on that. "The paras are ready to bring in hundreds of reinforcements," he assures me.

To the lawyer it seems obvious that the police must be mighty relieved that the *autodefensas* are here at last. The gangs killed two police last year, yet juveniles (less than eighteen years old) are protected by law. They cannot be imprisoned, and the worst punishment they face is reform school for short periods of time, maybe eighteen months, he says, even for murder. Hence, as with so much Colombian justice and its enlightened laws, the actual law is assassination.

Like water spiraling down a funnel, our conversation eventually reaches the topic of Carlos Alfredo Díaz, the squatter settlement at the end of town. As I listen to his rant, I ask myself, Can it be a real place? Brushing aside my incredulity, he insists it is stupendously dangerous. It dawns on me that just as the guerrilla have their most important base in the endless forests of the Caquetá, at the end of nowhere on the edge of the Amazon basin, so the gang world of youth gone wild has its sacred grove, too, right here on the urban edge, where the slums hit the cane fields at Carlos Alfredo Díaz.

There are trails, he says, concealed in the cane fields connecting CAD with a flat-topped mountain several miles due north along the valley floor. The mountain is called Navarro, and it rises from the plains at the southern edge of Cali. Entirely artificial, this mountain is made of garbage. All the city's garbage goes there. Face furrowed with anxiety, he tells me Navarro is even worse than CAD, and people walk between the two places to escape other gangs and the law. CAD has a flourishing market in drugs and weapons, but the mountain an even bigger one.

Night is falling. The lightbulb is a dull orange glow. The plastic lounge chairs and the cold tiled floor offer little comfort. As we talk, my stomach contracts. It is a rare pleasure to be able to speak at length and in such a calm, measured way with someone from the town who knows so much about the inner workings of its administration. We have met two times before: once in his house two years ago, and once, early morning bleary-eyed, in the police station, where he gave an incisive talk to the police on human rights (which the police chief welcomes, identifying such rights as meaning little more than obeying the police). Yet it is his forced calm that makes me anxious. We have hit bedrock. There is nowhere to hide, emotionally or logically. It is unusual, I think, in this culture, for just two men to be conversing alone and intensely like this. It feels secretive and dangerous. He makes me afraid with his fear, tempered as it is by his probity. Everyone here is frightened of the paras and of the possibility they will acquire total power. People are also frightened—in fact, extremely frightened—of a counterattack by the guerrilla. Our voices get lower in case anyone overhears. Without letting the other see, we sneak glances at the twelve-foot-high cement wall running through the living room space, dividing us from the house next door. Why do we let our glances steal in that direction? Is it because we wonder if someone is eavesdropping? My body tightens. I feel trapped in this cement box of a house. He is a steady, methodical talker, hearing himself through me, a stranger from the U.S., on whom he can try out his ideas and feel reassured in some way. But his steadfastness unnerves me. Sounding logical is our only defense. Maybe I am his lightning rod, ready to absorb the worst. Several times he says, "This is worse than a dictatorship."

In his opinion, the local businesspeople did not invite these killers. Instead, they are forced to collaborate. They are pressured for money for arms and motorbikes, for cellular phones and daily living costs. The *autodefensas* see a car or a pickup. "Here! Give me the keys!" The *autodefensas* see a house empty for rent and they move in without paying, leaving the TO RENT sign on the wall. Anyone who owns a car now keeps it locked up out of sight.

Worst of all, in his opinion, is that he has heard through the grapevine that members of the town board opposed to the current mayor secretly went to the *autodefensas* to solicit their aid in holding a trial of the mayor for corruption. The *autodefensas* told the mayor where and when he had to meet them—no ifs, and, or buts. He faced his accusers, denied any wrongdoing, insisted the way to raise such complaints was with the legal authorities, and the meeting broke up with the *autodefensas* saying they would scrutinize the municipal records and get back to him.

Yet this is precisely what the guerrilla have been doing for a decade or longer. It is said that the guerrilla now have control of roughly one third of Colombia's 1,100 municipalities. In 1985 they were said to be active in 170 municipalities. Ten years later

the figure had jumped to 622. As the basic unit of state administration, the municipality is now responsible for its own budget
and income, with authority vested in a mayor and twelve coun-
selors, nowadays elected by popular vote, with regular monthly
public meetings. Some of these municipalities may be manifestly
in the hands of the guerrilla, but more common is an indirect
rule, whereby local elections are held with the guerrilla in the
background, quietly keeping a close watch on who is put forward
as a candidate and on what and how honestly the budget is spent.
It seems like the Colombian countryside is being divided up between the paras and the guerrilla, leaving the state as a baroque
facade. Gone are the days when revolution demanded you attack
and acquire the symbols of sovereignty such as the presidential
palace, congress, and whatever else constitutes the sacred center
of the nation-state.

Yet long before the guerrilla and the *autodefensas* started to
control local government, Colombian municipalities were run
the same way, with a semi-secret group of local businessmen
calling the shots, in webs of intrigue with state officials. Such
groups are deeply institutionalized—the state within the state—
and even have a name, La Rosca, referring to a doughnut-shaped
pastry with its hollow center. So what's new? Well, the use of
overt violence is new, that's true, but it was always there, really,
hovering in the wings. What stays the same, the very same, is the
hollow center we can never get to know. The *rosca*. What a challenge for those who want "transparency" in government. How
do you make a void transparent?

Waiting in the airport the day I left Colombia, a week after my conversation with the lawyer, I read a long article by Fabio Castillo in the national Colombian newspaper, *El Espectador,* reporting that paramilitaries in cahoots with groups of drug traffickers have taken over Tumaco, the second largest port on the Pacific coast. Lying on stinking mudflats in suffocating heat on the border with Ecuador, Tumaco, population 150,000, is pretty well isolated from the rest of Colombia but for one treacherous road snaking its way down the Andes. Coca for cocaine and poppies for heroin are now being grown on that side of the *cordillera,* coca and poppies that are fought over by the guerrilla and several Cali drug cartels. Hence the arrival of the paras. Fabio Castillo tells us of the soldier from the regular army in a red beret filming passengers as they get off the daily flights, presumably to identify and intimidate them. He relates how in only three days last September (2000) the paras wiped out all the youth gangs in Tumaco. Following this, the paras exiled or killed all the beggars, and in the last three months have been pursuing labor leaders and those whom the journalist designates as "political independents." But nobody will talk. At least not to the journalist. Nobody even knows where to find the grave of Flavio Bedoya, another journalist assassinated by men on motorbikes a few blocks from the police station. He wrote an anonymous article for the Communist Party's newspaper *La Voz,* noting the participation of a regular army officer in a paramilitary assault on a village in the region that was important in the drug trade. On condition of anonymity, a district attorney summed up the situation: "The operation is similar to what the paras do in any other city. First there's an operation of social prophylaxis, to gather community support. Then they kill independent voices, of whom there are few here anyway." In this article the motives are clear, and everything seems to make sense. But from where I stand, it would be difficult to write a report like that.

Months later a young woman, the girlfriend of a paramilitary leader on the Pacific coast, explained to me how simple it all was. There are three things the paras do, she said. Exterminate the guerrilla, which means exterminate the people who support them. Second, control the drug trade. And third, "social control"—which is, I guess, what was going on in our town. Yet this merely exchanged one puzzle for another. I no longer had to categorize the activities of the paras as either drug trafficking or counter-guerrilla warfare. But what exactly is "social control" and why do the paras want it?

MAY 22

LISTLESS AND BORED, I go to the market, a fraction the size it was ten years ago. It is hot and fly-ridden. In the roofed-over section I see the men butchers in their dirty white aprons, lifting like tents over their bulging stomachs. The women butchers, long and lean, known as *triperas,* occupy the other side of the aisle, but the flies and heavy smell of fat are the same. While the men sell the outsides, red meat, beef and pork, the women sell the insides, brains, liver, small intestines, half skulls smashed open with torn flesh, a blue eye bulging. The men have their meat hung vertically from shiny hooks. I once read of paramilitaries arriving by helicopters to a series of villages situated on the grass plains that extend toward Venezuela, where they suspended their victims for several days from hooks such as these in an abattoir before killing them. The local military commander said he knew nothing about it.

L. insisted I lunch at her place two blocks from the market. She serves me two fish heads. One lands in my lap. I take off my pants and her nineteen-year-old daughter scrubs them outside on a broken piece of concrete slab by the toilet, a hole in the ground, which has a ragged piece of hemp bag on a nail for a door. We eat in the darkness of the kitchen. Her son R. died here at age twenty-eight from stomach cancer a few years back in the front room, unable to eat for weeks before he died. Resourceful, honest as the day is long, handsome, and strong, he made a sort of a living selling potatoes, following the local markets. On his days off he sold lottery tickets in Cali, at the most sixty a day, amounting to two U.S. dollars for himself. I lent him money for drumming lessons from a woman teacher in Cali whose brother got imprisoned in the U.S. for trafficking.

R. once told me about his military service in the early 1980s in Palmira, a large agricultural town close to Cali, where at one point he was instructed in assassination. His unit wore civilian clothes, grew their hair longer than regulation, studied photographs of persons to be killed, tracked them secretly during the day, and trained to shoot from motorbikes with a pillion rider. He learned to torture captured guerrilla. "They do it to us, so we do it to them." His officers lectured the troops: "Communism is evil. Not democratic." When he was discharged he looked for work in construction in Cali. It was boom-time then, with cocaine money, and Pinski's construction company was having a ball tearing up and reconstructing the city. Later, Pinski went bankrupt, as did most everybody else, but even in the boom-time R. couldn't get a job for longer than twenty-eight days, that being the minimum to qualify for social security payments, and the wage barely covered his costs for transport and lunch. Some democracy. Nowadays a young man like that would be likely to join the paras.

His mother L. and I became friends shortly after I first arrived in the town, in December 1969. We met through her grandfather, a gentle giant in his eighties who answered my questions about local history with epic poems in rhyming verse he composed himself and knew by heart no matter their length. He had never attended school and had taught himself to read as a child, but had been blind for many years, sitting in the sun explaining things to me in his high-pitched, quavering voice, poems tugging at his elbow.

Tengan presentes senores, lo que voy a contar.
A los enemigos de los pobres, no los deben olvidar.

Listen hard my friends, to what I'm about to recite.
The enemies of the poor, you must never let out of sight.

I was surprised by a long poem he'd made up about the *Violencia* of the 1940s and 1950s. It was no less comic than tragic. Everyone, and not only the government and its soldiers, its police and its paramilitaries (then known as *chulavitas*), ended up looking pretty silly—a far cry from the poetry of the literate classes, full of romance and pathos, or the sentimentality of the poetry of the young people in the town today.

Blessed God, what is to be done
about the government of Zambrano?
We are like two beasts, brother killing brother.
Since Zambrano came, we felt the chill.
They stripped us bare and began to kill.

Oh! My! What a time for the black folk!
With a gun at the door:
"Hands up, you fuckers!
Your courage has gone,
You don't dare to fight.
Screw black people,
and the Liberal Party, too.
Long Live Doctor Laureano Gómez,
Elected president of Colombia!
With the military police and chulavitas *now arm in arm,*
We are going wipe out even your shadow.

After many verses this poem ended:

Now surely they will kill me because I always tell the truth,
Because my pen keeps writing, even when I stop to think of proof.
And if, because of my verses, enemies come aswarming,
I feel all the stronger, and not only on account of this warning.
And by the way, I must inform you, I never had a teacher.
Yet as you know a tiger from its stripes,
So you get to know a person from the shape their writing takes,
Here stop the verses written by my hand [mano]
Thus came—and went—the government of Marco Polo Zambrano.

For many years I thought his granddaughter—my good friend L.—had the inside dope on everything. She was my weathervane, registering otherwise invisible currents running through the social world. We formed a theater, she and I, fabulist and audience together. Often a scratchy transistor radio would be switched on, and I think a good deal of her gossip actually came from that source, imprinted of course with her language and emphatic gestures. But as time went on I became perplexed at how many things supposedly going on in town she either didn't know about or she didn't set aflame with her sense of high drama and love of secrecy. Maybe her life had just gotten too rough after her son died. Maybe it was me who was melodramatic and greedy for sensational stories and I was outpacing her. Or maybe she and I have different wavelengths that sometimes engage and sometimes don't. Nevertheless it was she who opened up for me a way of thinking about the art of confusion in relation to violence and inner life.

This sensitivity to the art—and politics—of confusion came on strong to me in the early 1980s, when I began to see the world in radically fractured ways that my training had not prepared me for. The Turbay government ordered frequent states of emergency and tortured prisoners arrested under new laws in response to increased guerrilla activity. In 1980, the recently formed M-19 guerrilla staged its spectacular robbery of the Colombian army's munitions supply by tunneling through the mountain behind Bogotá on New Year's Eve, leaving a note: "Happy New Year—and Happy New Arms." My life was in disarray. I was separating from my wife. My mother had just died. I remember staying with the Jesuits in Bogotá and sleeping in the attic, watching faces pass across the rafters at four in the morning. And that was my moment of peace. Everything was falling apart. M-19 friends were hiding, on the run, and being tortured. Preparing a book on the rubber boom in the upper Amazon and trying to figure out a way of talking about hallucinogenic healing of sorcery in that same region, I would visit the shamans in the Putumayo, days in a bus with the moon swinging now through the back windows, now through the sides, as the empty bus took the curves over the mountains to Pasto and thence over the ghostly *páramos* down the mountains to Mocoa, where, huddled against the cold and spewing our hearts out, poor colonists and myself were beholden to an old Indian singing with the angels, laughing and crying our way through that crackling voice. This was also a time when instability and contradiction were beginning to be valued—not devalued—by some of us working in the human sciences which, up to that point, had been geared to making sense of the social world as if it were like a machine responding to high pressure and low pressure, like the plumbing of a house, or the like the plot of a nineteenth-century novel with its beginning, middle, and end. But that version of reality was not the hallucinatory one we were facing.

Nor is it the reality in which the paramilitaries work and magnify. No way. They are laughing all the way to the next massacre. The *limpieza* has nothing to do with that simplistic world, nor did the burgeoning guerrilla movement, nor the movement of fear and crime in the back streets of the small rural towns where L. was showing me the ropes with that deadly tongue of hers, making me aware of what I came at first to call the world of "multiple realities." I still have the file of notes I kept under that heading, motivated as much by the different renderings of reality I came across as by my sinking confidence in being able to render that reality adequately.

This became still more puzzling when I learned to return to my notes and use them just as they were for their freshness of expression. I found I wanted to interpolate these heterogeneous nuggets of reality into the more artificial fabric I was weaving and allow them their outspoken presence regardless. All this came to be part of what I then called "multiple realities," a dull phrase, to be sure, but redolent with power as far as I was concerned, meaning heterogeneity as reality, the world a cosmic jigsaw puzzle with parts missing and others that will never fit. *Multiple realities.* A new way, for me, a new way of thinking about the situation, not to mention my place in it. Take the question of the corpses found lying by the road in 1982, according to notes I wrote at that time:

M.R.'s

Squadrons of Death/Cadavers: December 3, 1982

H. and T. told me today there were some ugly things the past months—namely dead bodies found every day on the mile of dirt road just out of town—but "it's gotten a lot better." It's a lonely stretch with scraggly trees and cattle pastures on either side. "Squadrons of death," says H. "Couldn't leave your house after 10:00 at night," says T.

I ask O., a store owner, and Mariza, a clerk, about these corpses. O. has never heard of such things in Colombia until now. She tells me a young high school student in Cali named Cambalache was found dead near town, along with the body of the leader of a trade union, with his lips and eyelids sewn together. Mariza says the killers pour sulfuric acid over the faces and fingertips of their victims. Overwhelmed by fear and fascination, once she gets going, she can't be stopped.

G., a bicycle repairman who became mayor of the town, says these killers are paramilitary police types that around here only kill *delincuentes,* not union leaders. In Medellín there exists the MAS ("Death to Kidnappers," organized by the cocaine cartel), and they do kill union leaders. He asserts that dead bodies around here are *not* disfigured.

A. tells me that in March this year a body was found on the road with her face disfigured by acid and bullet holes in her body. A taxi driver found another rotting body by a cane field—*bastante podrido, ojos podridos.* He has never heard of Cambalache or of eyes sewn together. On one roadway there were about eight bodies found in one month. On another, two bodies were found with a message, and five more were found there, too. Some people say it is the doing of the police. Others say mafia. Still others say it is for revenge. A. thinks it is mainly the work of mafia, but offers this example: You rob the store of someone; someone else sees you and tells the store owner. You get to hear of this and kill the informer.

A.'s uncle (works in garbage collection) tells me there is no disfigurement. It is the sun and the rain weathering the faces, not acid. The faces get discolored, and the eyes and mouth puff up so it looks like acid and that they have been sewn together. All the killed were delinquents or it was done for revenge.

Or. and G. (university students) say the whole point of the variety of stories is to create uncertainty. They think it's exaggerated. It's the mafia that sews the eyes and mouth ("symbols," says G); acid is what the *políticos* do.

Back to T., horrified with all these bodies. Has heard of the acid, but not the sewing. When I ask people about the purpose of the acid, they say it's so the body can't be identified. But, I ask, wouldn't it be more effective if the body were identifiable?

JG (university student, sober and penetrating analyst) is emphatic on the need for terror. He is clear on who is behind the killings: "Don't you know it's these right-wing death squads?" I challenge him: "If the country is run by the military, as you say it is, and if the police are quite open with their brutality, as you say they are, why then would there be a need for clandestine death squads?" His answer: to get around human rights (which in 1982 barely existed).

Fair enough, but then I think of his mother and the brazen behavior of the police. JG was with a crowd of people at the scene of an accident in the street. A cop pushed him, saying he shouldn't be there. JG said he had every right to be there, and the cop confiscated his push-bike. Next day, JG had to travel to the town of Palmira, so his mother went to the police station to reclaim his bike. The cops said she had to pay 200 pesos. She asked why and refused to pay. They beat her, cursed her out, and her body is covered with bruises.

Elbia, a peasant woman who lives out of town, says she, too, has heard of corpses, acid, but no sewing. Probably mafia. Two years ago two guys came here in a car asking for a young man down the road. A good kid. They said they were taking him to Cali. To jail. But they killed him on the road and left his body there.

G., the bicycle repairman-mayor, understands what I mean by a "culture of terror." The principal problem, he says, is psychological, and the principal arm of the culture of terror is unemployment.

That night I was at H. and T.'s place at a village two miles down the road from the town. There were eight of us, including many of T.'s sisters and their husbands. I was struck by the gentleness of the men playing with the small kids. T.'s seventy-year-old father was there, too. He was working as a cane cutter till he became an invalid a year ago, at which point the sugar plantation denied him his pension on the grounds he had joined their workforce when he was more than sixty years old. I started talking about Elbia, who works as a field hand and earns so little, there is no food on Fridays, has to work on fiesta days without extra pay, and so forth. As we talk I feel the fear the conversation brings to life yet dispels at the same time—fear of killings, fear of hunger, fear of losing a job. It's not simply that they make a lot of jokes about a lot of things as well as tease one another. It's not simply that there is a rhythm, like a circle, in which each person becomes a character. It's that death and humor alternate in this circle and keep changing places.

There was a sanitation engineer working on a project here imprisoned by the army as an M-19 guerrilla. Released two months back, he went to reclaim his car and was shot dead by the intelligence service of the army known as the F-2.

People in the room express wonder about the M-19 guerrilla being made up of middle-class professionals who could live comfortably without risking their lives like this. The revolutionaries do it because they believe in equality, the people in the room tell me. They cannot get over this. It seems so unbelievable. "And is it true," asks one of T.'s sisters, "that there is such a thing as a lie detector?" Everyone laughs, then looks to me to provide the answer.

I ask T.'s sisters, What do the older people in this village say about the killings? They say it's the same old *Violencia*— the Liberals versus the Conservatives. They say it's the Apocalypse.

José's father, from the rivers in the jungles of the Chocó along the Pacific coast, is a cane cutter and loader who has been living here twenty years. He is skinny as a rail, with muscles defined in his shoulders like straps of leather, biceps that move up and down like square blocks of wood, a body barely recognizable as such, a body become a machine adapted to the work of the cane; later it will crack along the spine. We are drinking *aguardiente* with the jovial blacksmith, who wears a leather apron and is in bare feet. Talk about an anachronistic profession! A blacksmith here in this sugar plantation town of slums and machines filling the streets with the rumble of sugarcane wagons. The blacksmith is testimony to an earlier epoch, when there were peasants and the peasants had ponies and the ponies were loaded with bags of cacao and coffee, bunches of plantains, and bags of oranges. Well, here we are, at the crossroads of the dying past and the dying future, the blacksmith and the cane-cutter. "The corpses?" says José's dad. "They are product of the mafia and the squadrons of death killing the people that couldn't keep their mouth shut." He puts his finger over his lips: "Understand!"

That was 1982. As I reread this now, I am amazed at how little seems to have changed in twenty years. The decisive difference is that what before was diffuse is now compacted into one source, and its anonymity is of a different order now that we know assassination is largely the work of the paras. But then, who or what are the paras? In *Prisoner of Love,* Genet writes that "the essence of theater is the need to create not merely signs but complete and compact images masking a reality that consists in absence of being. The void." [9] And that's how the paras come across in this town. A void that kills.

The brazenness of the killing today takes your breath away, in broad daylight, in the street—the exact opposite of anonymity. This is not some remote hamlet where there are no police or law courts. This is a town just forty-five minutes by road from Cali, with 40 police, 5 judges, 3 district attorneys, a jail with 120 prisoners, and an elaborate judicial system. The triumph of the paras over all this is extraordinary. And here they are, hunkered down with the girls in El Cupido.

And of course other things have changed since those truly anonymous killings of the 1980s. The FARC guerrilla formed a legal political party, the Unión Patriótica, in 1985, but by 1995 paras had assasinated somewhere between two and three thousand of its members, including senators and two presidential candidates. Any assessment of the FARC's strategy, in particular its willingness to negotiate a just peace, must take this terrible fact into account. They cannot come in from the cold. They will be killed.

Then there is the arrival of the drug trade and the corruption it stimulates, a world of lies and secrets. At the same time the FARC has had great success in recruiting young peasants, girls as well as boys, and gained stupendous income from kidnapping and from taxing coca to pay those recruits. In 1996, the FARC's annual income was calculated at around $800 million U.S. Much of this is invested outside of Colombia, since there is more than enough money for this experienced guerrilla army to outfight the Colombian army on every front. Yet these activities, combined with a single-minded pursuit of military objectives—such as murdering policemen in isolated outposts—have led to an enormous loss of popular support for the FARC, including that of intellectuals, while during these past few years the paras' popularity has soared. Notable, too, has been the recently established U.S. "Plan Colombia," making Colombia the third largest recipient of U.S. military aid after Israel and Egypt. Yet to date, despite close to $2 billion in military hardware from the U.S., the Colombian government has scored no significant military success in its war against the FARC or drug trafficking.

But what about the violence? Surely that has gotten worse? The political scientists tell me that there was relatively little violence between the guerrilla and the state from 1960 to 1982. And my memory of the 1970s, for instance, is one of bucolic calm, being able to walk anywhere, town or country, floating free with the beauty of western Colombia, that scent like burning thyme in the foothills, the clouds tumbling over the mountains, dark blue and heavy with unfathomable mystery. But now the bug has caught me, and I want to return farther and farther back in time, and I am surprised at how much I have forgotten and my perspective altered. For when I look at my diaries for 1970–1972, I get a shock. I see first of all that my definition of "violence" is quite different. Instead of in-your-face knives and guns and corpses alongside the roads just outside of town, I see another class of violence, that by men against women, and second the violence of the economy with its unemployment, miserable pay, and humiliating working conditions. We could even conclude that, given the unique constellation of events that transpired during the decades following 1970, these more basic forces are what gave rise to the actual physical violence that I am writing about in my diary of a *limpieza* in 2001. The violence of the economy and that between the sexes gives way to the blatantly political and criminal violence, which in turn gives way to routine and numbness punctuated by panic.

Is this why keeping a diary is important? Coming home, I turn the pages of my diaries from the 1970s. They awaken memories, and I am scared by how much I have forgotten, not simply discrete events but the overall feeling of the time. I do not think this is as dramatic as the word "repression" might signify, when we use that word to describe the act of sealing off unpleasant memories from consciousness and then witlessly get caught by their unexpected return. Rather it's more like something being worn away through use, like the elbow of a coat, the knee of a pair of blue jeans, or an old and much-used knife whose cutting edge becomes curved and worn from years of sharpening. Here, history lies in the absence; in the cloth that's been worn, in the hole in the knee, and in the smooth arc of the cutting edge. Even more than in the absence, history lies in the adaptation of materials to time, to the exigencies of life, much as a door handle loses its shine or the keys on a keyboard lose their lettering.

What catches my eyes reading these old notes for 1970–1972 is the fear of thieves and of violence. This fear is everywhere like the beating of your heart night and day. If it stops, it means you've stopped.

When Guillermo killed Marlene and then immediately shot himself dead through the ear in 1972, hordes of people ran into their house, first to ogle, then to steal. That's what I was told, although the phrasing is my own. First to ogle, then to steal. Crowds surge to the emergency room of the hospital across the bridge when a victim of a violent crime is in his or her last agony.

The young tailor Julián assures me in 1971 that the reason for the switch from cattle to sugar in the valley mid-twentieth century is because cattle are too easy to steal. Sugar is the biggest thing to hit the valley since the Spanish Conquest. And to Julián, this switch came about because of fear of theft! How would a Marxist react to this explanation of the change in the mode of production? L.'s neighbor was highly pleased when a populist mayor was able to force the sugarcane back from the side of town she lived on. Why was she pleased? I assumed it was part of our messianic struggle against landlords and capitalism. No! Not at all! It was because the cane afforded innumerable places for thieves to hide. Whereas for us university radicals, the cane was the thief.

In April 1971, I record: Another murder last night. This makes the second in five days. It occurred in the main plaza about midnight. A young man was shot by another young man. It was "about a woman." The person killed was unarmed. The other murder occurred at the end of town close by the *"zona de toleran-*

cia" about eleven in the morning. I was walking around the corner when I saw a thick-set young man running disjointedly with both hands pressed to his stomach from which blood was spurting onto the street. He ran into Salomé's home and I followed. He lay down on a bed, but Salomé and Carmen want him outside. Quick! Eventually they get their way. He is carried out onto the pavement, where about thirty people are gathered, mainly kids and women. I try to get people to take him to the hospital, but there is no response. Don René, who owns the store on the corner, arrives, asks questions, agrees we should get him to the hospital, then backtracks along the trail of blood to find where it started. A few minutes later the man dies as I am hailing a truck a couple of blocks away to take him to the hospital. I am finding it difficult to get the driver to do this. He wants to come, but only to look, not to help. Suddenly a cry goes up: *"¡La Ley! La Ley!"* The police are coming. The onlookers scatter. Later it is explained to me that nobody can afford to help because being associated in any way with such a corpse can make you a suspect. Either you get carted off to jail immediately or else you get questioned continuously and then get into someone else's bad books because they suspect you have squealed on them. But I distinctly remember to this day thirty years later a collection for money begun outside Salomé's home to buy a coffin for the dead man. An immigrant cane-cutter or loader from the Pacific coast, he was a stranger. He had no kin here. And it would be unjust if the last rites were not observed. This is the justice everyone can agree upon.

Old María Cruz, leaning on her crutch, attending a pot on the fire in 1970 in her mud hut out in the countryside, tells me that it was probably a friend who stole my radio. "Happens all the time," she says. "That's why people make friends. To rob you."

A week later I meet Felipe Carbonera walking barefoot from his home of sticks. He is extremely old, and I talk to him quite often as he remembers his grandmother's stories about slavery. He is on his way to visit a spiritual healer so as to find out who stole his radio and get it back. The moral: Friends are the ones who rob you. Avoid the police, go to a spiritualist instead.

In September 1970, I heard that several parents in town received letters from persons threatening to kidnap their children if they didn't pay 5,000 pesos per child, a huge sum. The third or fourth person thus contacted called in that section of the national police—the DAS (whom people refer to as the secret police)—and made a dummy payment to a girl in Cali, from whom the DAS extracted several names of accomplices, one of whom worked in the town administration. National statistics indicate that kidnapping (at least that which was brought to the attention of the police) barely existed from 1960 through to 1990, when it suddenly took off. However, my diaries present a more complicated picture. Indeed, contrary to my memory, kidnapping seems far from being a recent development, and even relatively poor people were victims. In 1970 I also heard of the kidnapping of the Swiss consul's son in Cali. The story I got was that the police froze the consul's bank account so he couldn't pay ransom, but he borrowed the money, paid the kidnappers, and the son walked free into the valley town of Buga, two hours north of

Cali. A few weeks later several people were arrested on suspicion of this crime and were shot "trying to escape." L. warns me—as early as 1970—that I should be careful of kidnappers "who will ask my government for money." They usually work for Fidel Castro, she tells me. "They are not of the common people. They arrive in fine clothes with ties and in fine cars. . . ." All of this, I'd forgotten.

With this in mind, the paras seem less something new than the latest actualization of longstanding fear, taking advantage of that fear to control the town as a whole. What the paras can come to represent, in other words, is a promise to use violence to stop violence, to use fear to stop fear—a fear that has been dancing in the back of people's minds for as long as I have known this town, since 1969.

But has there been anything like the paras before in living memory? Historians advise, for instance, that in the 1930s the large landowners in the valley had their private police to deal with cattle rustling, which, so it is said, because of the misery of the great depression, had reached "alarming levels."[10] But to grasp the importance of this, one has to consider politics. Elections by means of secret ballot have long existed in Colombia, and up until 1949 the valley was, by and large, a Liberal Party stronghold. Left-wing ideas were making great strides amongst the rank and file of that party, and this, together with a growing Communist Party and Communist guerrilla organization fermenting among coffee growers in the eastern highlands of Colombia since the 1930s,

threw the Conservative Party into a frenzy. In those days the
two-party system was based on mutual hatred, with each party,
quite apart from its ideological values, animated by what they
called a *mística,* a "mystique," akin to religious passion, that is
probably impossible for outsiders, such as myself, to understand.
Moreover, the party that held the presidency, as the Conservatives did in 1946, after twenty years of Liberal hegemony, also
controlled the appointment of the governors at the regional level
as well as the mayors of the municipalities and most other admin-
istrative positions. When the *Violencia* broke out with the assassination of the Liberal Party leader, Gaitan, the ninth of April,
1948, the Conservatives controlled the state. In 1949 the Conservative governor of the Cauca valley called in leading cattlemen
and hacienda owners, asking them to subsidize a private police
force, initially 300 men strong, which would be the armed wing
of the Conservative Party aimed at a type of ethnocide, eliminating the Liberal Party throughout the valley.[11] Local branches of
the Conservative Party, particularly in the prosperous little
towns of the foothills in the north and center of the valley,
formed death squads. Known as "birds," or *pájaros,* with leaders
such the Condor, the Vampire, Blue Bird, and Green Bird, these
were urban-based groups of assassins famous for their black
"phantom cars" without registration plates. Feared over half the
valley, the Condor was a small man running a cheese stall in the
market of the small town of Tulua well to the north of Cali. Described as honest and hardworking, a devout Catholic much
given to prayer, he had made a name for himself grabbing dyna-
mite and an ancient shotgun to defend a local chapel supposedly

threatened by the Liberal "hordes"—the infamous *chusma* or rabble.

The *pájaros* functioned semi-secretly from 1949 into the mid-1950s with the support of local government institutions such as town boards, the judiciary, the jails, and the secret services of intelligence of the state.[12] After that, despite changes in politics at the national level, and with many of the big *pájaros* killed—some by other *pájaros*, the Condor by the son of one his Liberal victims—it is alleged that the institution of the *pájaros* nevertheless forced peasants off land to make way for sugar plantations in the 1960s, while in the early 1970s they are reputed to have acted against the Indian organization, CRIC, of the central highlands, as well as against peasants involved in land invasions in the valley organized by ANUC, the national peasant organization.[13]

Within a few months of their formation in late 1949, the *pájaros* had so frightened people that many, like the Jews in the Spanish Inquisition, formally converted to the Conservatives. It is astonishing how quickly this happened. It took but three to four months, such that what had been a Liberal fortress before 1946, namely the Cauca Valley, became an electoral bulwark of the Conservatives after 1949. The *pájaros* murdered important Liberals, railway workers, and trade union leaders. Together with masked police in October 1949, the *pájaros* effected a wholesale slaughter of twenty-six members of the Liberal Party leadership in their headquarters in the very center of Cali, and it is significant—highly significant—that the national army took three hours to get to the scene of the massacre.[14]

To get a sense of the curious interplay between police and

paramilitary elements, let me quote the following story from a local valley newspaper in October 1949:

> In Restrepo, armed civilians belonging to the Conservative Party followed the command of the *jefe ilegal* of the Party— i.e., the commander of the *pájaros*. Often they would be accompanied by two or three police. At other times these same civilians would dress up as police in uniforms made by a well-known tailor with the consent of the authorities. Plundering, robbery, arson, and assassinations were carried out by these groups whom, with their "lieutenants" and "sergeants," took away IDs and dynamited the homes of Liberals.[15]

What is striking and indeed hard to understand is the theatrical, even childish, nature of the deceit. More an open secret than a true secret (in the local newspaper!), it seems it was intended as an absurd charade, hence all the more terrifying. Just like today.

Even the national police, created by the Conservative Party with the outbreak of *La Violencia* in 1948, were themselves a sort of paramilitary force, stormtroopers feared by Liberals who called them *chulavitas,* referring to the fanatically loyal Conservative Party peasants from eastern highland towns such as Chulavita, who quickly replaced local police in many parts of the country at the beginning of *La Violencia.*

Twenty-two years later, in 1970, Luis Carlos Carabali, a landless laborer, told me about the arrival of the *chulavitas* as a paramilitary force in the town that my diary concerns, a town like so many in the valley with a massive Liberal majority. He had just the right style. Sweeping his arms in grand gestures, squatting low to the ground, with his sharp-looking felt hat on all the time, he imitated people and evoked scenes from the past. He died around 1995.

At the time of the ninth of April [1948] I was living in Pitalito. In the afternoon, news swept through about the death of Gaitán and that there were people taking things out of the shops in town and so I went and I took. People were grabbing bottles of rum, snapping off the tops, taking mouthfuls, then smashing the bottle still full of liquor onto the street.

"You couldn't walk in bare feet for at least a week," interjected María Cruz.

Man it was a party! Then we heard the police were coming. I wasted no time. We fled. At that time there was no road, only a narrow path leading from town to Pitalito. The police, and later the *chulavitas,* were too scared to go along it because there was always a peasant ready to shoot if he could get away with it. Airplanes flew over the town exploding bombs but pretty harmlessly, just to scare us, you know, but when the troops got to town a day or so later they did kill quite a few people. And others fled the same as me. As soon as we heard that the police and the army were on their way and had blocked off all roads leading out of town, everyone ran to the forest. Out where we lived we were pretty safe. Now and again a rumor would race around that the *chulavitas* were on their way. Once at night there were some shots and everyone was sure they were coming. All the families fled into the night carrying their most precious belongings into the forest. As they couldn't use candles, because that would betray their presence, many stumbled and fell, encumbered as they were with bundles of clothes and whatever else. The others would keep running past, and that person would have to do their best on their own. We were scared shitless.

His mother-in-law, María Cruz, joined in. "One night the *chulavitas* came out here. We knew they were coming and the men-folk ran away into the night because if they were found they would surely be killed. I was left alone in the house with the children. The *chulavitas* knocked on the door. I said, "Wait a minute." But they smashed down the back door, fifteen to twenty of them asking for the guns. That was what they were always looking for: arms. They picked up the end of the bed on which the kids were sleeping and threw them into a corner. They took all the money in the house and left." María Cruz began to shake—like a tree in a storm, she said.

MAY 23

L. WAS RAISED BY NUNS in a convent where she got a harsh view of the world. In Cuba, naked people pull the plows. That sort of thing. She believed it. I met her in 1970, and she immediately impressed me with her fear. She was always telling me to take off my watch when I walked through the streets, for example, otherwise the *rateros,* meaning the thieves and the hoodlums, would have me for breakfast. She is a big woman, with a slight stoop that makes her look grim and determined. When we walked through the streets, she would look straight ahead and talk through one side of her mouth: "Look! See that guy lounging on the corner? He's a murderer." And she would give me the gory details. Better than a police file. Because her manner was so melodramatic, I assumed she exaggerated the amount of crime. But because of the exaggerations, I think she was able to convey the grain and the feel of what was actually going on. She was an artist.

Her daughter X., age nineteen, is from another planet, the way she fades in and out of reality. Small in build, like her father, she is volatile, eccentric, utterly impractical, yet blessed with a dashing sense of dress and, like her mother, a great singing voice. Her father, from the Chocó rain forest, just south of Panamá, came here as a migrant cane-worker in the 1960s. After a few years he left for higher-paying Venezuela to cut cane and, after that, via helicopter, to look for gold in the Venezuelan Amazon.

X. drifts, too, but only in her mind, like stardust. When she speaks, the world accelerates like a movie in fast motion and that's why it is such fun being with her. For a long time after her brother died she slept in the room in which he'd died that horrible, slowly starving death from stomach cancer. Sleeping in his bed, X. tossed and turned. A shadow would emerge from the closet. She had headaches, lost her energy, even her will to live. Her mother thought it was sorcery performed by the woman opposite whose daughter had died in childbirth and believed L. did that with sorcery. What was happening to X., therefore, could be construed as payback.

So, I did something outrageous. I tried to cure X., relying on my time with Indian shamans in the far-off Putumayo region of the upper Amazon. I went out into the countryside and picked some rustling leaves with which to make a curing fan, as I had been taught. I bought a bottle of *aguardiente*, then went to see the herbalist in the marketplace, a man born and raised in the Putumayo, and asked his advice on herbs, which I packed into the *aguardiente*. But when I returned to the house to perform the healing at 4:30 in the afternoon, X. was not there! So much for my self-importance! "I am playing God," I wrote in my 1997 diary. "I am an Indian medicine man. At last! After all those years in medical school in Sydney."

While waiting, I talked with her stepfather. God only knows what he thought of this strange intervention—a gringo trying to be an Amazonian Indian curing sorcery destroying a young black woman. He told me of the recent kidnapping by the guerrilla of two of the owners of the sugar plantation that dominates this region and employs him. The guerrilla kidnapped one of the owners recently, along with his teenage son. I wonder if these poor Jews fleeing the Soviet Union had any idea that these terrible things would happen to them as payback when they started acquiring the lands of these black peasants for their plantation in the 1950s? It must have all been so easy at first, acquiring lands hand over fist from peasants who rarely had title and were easily seduced by offers of cash. But now, with the guerrilla . . .

X.'s stepfather speaks in a quiet singsong signaling neither pleasure nor malice, but I know many here who were delighted at the thought of the owner having to perform the sort of manual labor they have to perform their entire lives. "He came back exhausted. They had him working like a young man. Now he is in Israel." His freedom cost the owners of the plantation *un poco de plata* (meaning "a lot of money") and better conditions for the workers as well as better pay. For instance, they now have to be brought back to town no later than five in the afternoon, and unpopular foremen and bosses had to be fired. The plantation had to invest more in the town's infrastructure as well. Two years ago the guerrilla threatened to burn tractors when the plantation fired twenty-two workers. As a result, the workers were reinstalled and everyone expects a pay raise. But X.'s mother, L., disapproves in general of the guerrilla because, she says, they don't respect human rights. She also disapproves of human rights groups because, while they are ready to heap blame on the paras, in her opinion they do not criticize the guerrilla for fighting dirty.

It took me two days to make some notes on the actual healing of X. What was I resisting? Why didn't I write? Well, first there's the actual fear of writing down what's happened. You feel you can never, ever, do justice to the complexity of events, and certainly not to the emotions raging. The best you can do is register a few images, maybe draw a diagram, and as the pen scrawls across the page your heart sinks because with each word you open up ever emptier spaces that not all the time or talent in the world could fill. And I was drained. When it was over I sat against the wall, smoked a cigarette, slowly walked home, bathed out back, and rested as if I'd run a marathon. Is this how the Indian shamans in the Putumayo feel? If so, it must be hard for them to maintain, as many of them do, their wonderful mix of toughness and tenderness in the space of death into which the healing opens, giggling inappropriately being an indispensable part of that voyage. But on the other hand they are part of a tradition and are surrounded by people similarly attuned. But me? I'm not only a novice. I'm a pioneer, as is X.

My singing was so deplorable! I almost stopped because of that and because I couldn't spray the medicine with my mouth in a fine shower over her face and head. It came out in great gobs. I must practice more!

I realize now how crucial is the creation of an "altered state of consciousness," with or without drugs. You have to create a scene of intense engagement with the spirits of the disease. Your singing and movements carry you to them and them to you. At least for that moment you have to believe in spirits, or believe in people who believe in spirits, and continue their work.

Is this what diary-writing is all about, too, writing not to yourself but to the spirits? I appreciate how pretentious this can sound, but then there is a real problem concerning the identity of the reader when it comes to a diary. You are writing to yourself, ostensibly, but everyone knows that at best this is nothing more than a convenient fiction, a strange convention linking selfhood to writing, built around the deeper problem of writing in general, no matter what form the writing takes. Even when totally absorbed in this fiction of writing to yourself, you can't avoid the horde of invisible readers looking over your shoulder.

Writers often say they have to imagine an audience for whom they are writing, but I doubt they can really visualize or be specific as to who or what constitutes this audience. There is a face, almost a face, swimming just beyond the metallic horizon of the typewriter keys or floating ghost-like in the gray waters of the computer screen. That audience and this face are actually the spirits without whom writing could not be.

Writing thereby turns out to be more than a communication between you and me. First and foremost it is a conversation with the spirits. This is to whom the shamans sing with their faces painted, rocking back and forth, while people like me, who are not shamans, merely writers, have only ghosts of spirits, spirits of spirits we can no longer figure with any confidence. The diary brings them even more forcefully to mind as elusive entities because of the intensity of its lonely labor.

All this makes life look so eventful. But it's not. Diaries record events, not non-events. Well, that's not true, either. Diaries record trivia, too. In doing so they fold life back on itself so we see the ordinary in new ways, especially on rereading.

"What I remembered best was what was not written, the interstices of notation," said Roland Barthes on rereading his diary. For instance he suddenly recalls the grayness of the atmosphere in the Rue de Rivoli while awaiting the bus there—precisely because it is *not* recorded in the diary entry he is rereading. "No use trying to describe it now, anyway," he adds, "or I'll lose it again instead of some other silenced sensation, and so on . . . role of the Phantom, of the Shadow."[16] It seems like there is a fascinating law here, a law of memory in relation to diary-writing: to record is to repress, yet rereading one's writing hauls the repressed into the mind's eye.

Which is all very well for a person rereading his own diary— playing musical chairs, as it were, with memory and the recording of memory, the one receding as the other steps forth. But what about me? And you? For I am rereading my diary notes with a view to telling you what happened and what it was like there in the town when the paras came. In my case, then, rereading has to mean a good deal of rerecording as well. Hence the diary-form slips step by wayward step into something else. What do we end up with then? A faux-diary, perhaps? Or a meta-diary? But names are not what's important here. What's important is what happens to the grayness of the Rue de Rivoli, to the interstices of memory made vivid precisely because, while they evade the writer, they animate the reading.

Falling way behind in my notes. All the important ideas and memories occur in flashes—like when I'm bathing out back in the tiny cement patio with glass chips on top of the walls. When you scoop the cold water out of the tub and feel it run down your head and shoulders, you travel for a few seconds to a beautiful faraway place like the seaside of memory where the world is sweet and fresh. Then things occur to me long after they've happened. The notes are not synchronous. I keep going back days later writing in the margins at an angle to the main text with these afterthoughts that are more like the real thoughts. The afterthoughts are not so much thoughts as memories, memories tagged to other memories like the outtakes littering the film editor's floor hauled jerkily over troughs of time. But then how different is a thought to a memory? They swim into focus with an image. These images get mixed up with when I was a child. The long ago and the now becomes the same as the far away and the here.

Freud has a stimulating discussion of this in an early paper entitled "Screen Memories," trying to uncover the place of the present in especially vivid memories we may have of our childhood. His concern is fresh and innocent. He is astonished how cunningly the picture-symbols of memory lie, how they can therefore be juxtaposed with present circumstance so as to create a sense of continuity and meaning to our lives, filling out the infinity of voids and pain. This is the deceit of art that vainly tries to add flesh to the bare bones of a diary, too, layering it with thoughts and afterthoughts. One could gently tease apart the layers and marvel at the cross-connections until they burst into this discussion one has with oneself about the doing of my doing no less than its undoing. And why is this urgent? Because in its delirium of screening, the diary replicates the finer weave of terror that the war machine aspires to.

It is not only a question as to whether the memories are true records of what happened. What is also important are the workings of memory and what such workings may reveal or stimulate. Language, as in the notes and afterthoughts that crisscross each other, becomes thus the theater of memory, not its instrument, such that the diary becomes more than mere record. Sometimes this palimpsest is called "surreality" or "magical realism" but whatever term we choose, it is the reality with which both the diary and terror function. Of course not all diaries do this. But all diaries have that potential where words and memories evoking other memories collide. What is crucial, however, is not surreality or magical reality but the movement, the trajectory back and forth across the divide that separates day from night.

One writer whose work is especially given over to visual images and memory said that as he got older his writing came to depend more and more on his memories of his childhood and adolescence. That was William Burroughs. But I believe that the treasure he excavates is not the long-ago of the magic of childhood, but the mottled screen of the screen memories, which as fabulous artistry weaves the present and the past together such that finally fiction is truer than fact. Let me put it like this: not the child, but the adult's imagination of the child; and not so much a picture or a word but a hieroglyph, which acts like a natural, even sacred, connection between text and image.

One of Burroughs's least-known contributions to literature was the diary in the form of a scrapbook. Hooked on junk in Tangier in the fifties, writing letters to close friends such as Allen Ginsberg that would come to form the core of *Naked Lunch*, Burroughs had described his technique as one of opening a cupboard drawer to expose the miscellany of things inside. Later in the early sixties in Paris he developed the scrapbook, which, to my mind, has some similarities to what I was doing as I kept my anthropologist's diary. Burroughs of course is seen as an artist while an anthropologist is seen as . . . well, an anthropologist. His scrapbook combined typewritten diary-type entries, paragraphs of "fiction," clippings from newspapers including the funnies, old black-and-white photos, and abstract designs painted onto blank space as well as onto the written material. Color leaps from the pages in a flurry compounded by typewritten words and curious, at times uncanny, photographic images. Clearly etched at the top of each page is the day and month of the year. "In cutting up you will get a point of intersection," commented Burroughs, "where the new material that you have intersects with what is there already in some very precise way, and then you start from there."[17] In a more scientific mood, Burroughs thought this could amount to a decoding operation practiced on the unconscious dimensions of dominant culture. This idea is close to the dream of an anthropologist analyzing the mythological dimensions of social control and, at the same time, doing something more than analysis, creating a new cultural force-field with the recording device itself.

Looking at the changing character of my own diaries over time, I am made aware how what at first was a diary co-existing with field notes and materials distributed into many categories such as history, land tenure, religion, and magic, a few years later was absorbed into nothing more than a diary into which I would glue clippings, photographs from newspapers, and leaflets, alongside my drawings and then layers of writings overlapping with and commenting on previous entries. At times the jumble of diary entries make just the sorts of connections Burroughs has in mind where he talks of an operation practiced on the unconscious dimensions of dominant culture.

But there is one more thing to account for, and this is the romance about fieldwork that people are quick to deflate. As a result, they come to devalue or even dismiss their afterthoughts and memories. For what I think happens is that being suspended between cultures, one disappears into childhood. Images never before recalled now flood one's being like the water I splash over my head out in the patio before going to sleep. Contaminated water. It runs down your body like fire from the stars as the memories run, too. Through similarity or contrast, these images mesh with recent experience so as to elicit aleatory significance, as with a basin full of water becoming the sea. Such images are inevitable and indispensably at the core of politics and war, not to mention the passions that fuel love. So this becomes more than an analysis. It becomes a way of working. To be hit by images magically sprung forth with a dash of cold water from a dish over one's head, to write afterthoughts at right angles in the margin, is to begin this process anew.

MAY 24

L. TELLS ME AT LEAST ONE of the killings the past five days were by paras in response to the murder of the store owner who lived across the road from her, the man who was shot though the liver in front of his kids and died after naming his murderers. He was liked by many people here, and the paras are determined to kill his killers. Hunting them down in the streets around her house, they shot an innocent man through the stomach by mistake. He was leaning against the corner of the street and looked like one of the killers. The bullet pierced his intestines, and now he's got a colostomy bag as he awaits further surgery. They tore down a front door with a pickax and crowbar late at night, but the killer they were pursuing escaped. Only the father was there, naked with a sheet around him, crying, "Assassinate me! Assassinate me! But out in the street!" They are cruising around here on motorbikes, the pillion rider with an automatic weapon.

The store owner's body was shipped out by his father to be buried in Buenaventura, where it is said his relatives performed magic on the corpse so the killers will be unable to flee the town, making them sitting ducks for the paras. The dead man's father lives in Buenaventura, famous here for its sorcerers, and is said to be furious with the way his relatives are handling things here.

I meet the dead man's mother and two sisters in their house across the road from L. and tell them how sorry I am. It's easier to say these things there than here, perhaps because death is no stranger, but mainly because the rituals for the dead are more in place. Formality provides the distance that allows one to come close. They are listless and overcome by the heat. L. insists I meet the other son, but I want to leave. She takes me by the hand to another room. There is a skinny man, age about thirty-five, lying on his back paralyzed from the neck down. He can't talk. A stroke, L. tells me in her matter-of-fact way. As we leave, she confides how bad-tempered he is with his mother, that he watches TV late at night and eats only when he wants to.

A friend wants me to write a letter to strengthen his application to the Canadian embassy for asylum in Canada, claiming he's been threatened by the paras. Several people here are doing the same. A mutual friend vents her frustration, saying he's no more threatened than anyone else. I recall my anthropologist friend who laughed when I asked if she was threatened. "Here in Colombia we are all threatened."

M. takes me to meet an ex-gangster friend of his by name of V. What makes an ex-gangster no longer a gangster? Indeed, is there such a thing as an ex-gangster? We walk through dark, empty streets and enter a house without knocking. Nobody looks surprised. Three guys are watching TV. One is jet-black with a shaven head, shirtless, age about twenty-two. This is V. We move onto the patio out back to have a private conversation. The patio is roofed over, with a truck taking up most of the space. We are joined by two young women, one buxom in scarlet pants who is V.'s *compañera,* while the other woman, I later learn, used to belong to the all-female gang called Las Pirañas. Another ex! I introduce myself as the author of a now legendary history of the abolition of slavery and its aftermath in this area, a cheap paperback published in 1975, used in the high schools and long out of print. They make no sign of recognition. I talk about my experience with sorcery in the Putumayo and say I'd like to know about magic in gang-life here. Funny. I had no idea I would say this when I walked through the door. Usually you ease yourself slow into a subject like this, so full of euphemisms and taboos. But with V., I feel this is the way to go. The two young women look curious. Later I realize such magic is not my interest at all, and that's why I could be so direct. Was I trying to impress them with my credentials? Mainly I just wanted to be with them. I need to get out of my cement bunker, and I need to know these gang people and see the world the way they do. I know I will fail to do that, but I must try because right or wrong, I feel they are the wave of the future, the crystal ball, the summation of history. That is the "magic" that draws me now as the world enters its adolescence of identity crises, violence, and mad mood swings as we try to tether the imagination to a few flapping rags of the real. In this regard I also think of my curing X., and I'm not so sure my declared interest in magic is just an excuse. Maybe I've turned a corner, no longer content to merely study magic.

Cool as the proverbial cucumber V. says, "Oh yes! After you've killed five or six people you have to get cured."

"Where? Cali, Putumayo . . . ?"

"No! In the coast."

"Buenaventura?"

"Yes! In Buenaventura there are persons who know."

"So why do you need to be cured?"

"Because the family of the dead are likely to do sorcery on you. . . . Cachama!" said V. "Now there's someone you could talk to! *¡El es lo más sencillo!* You can talk to him direct. *Tiene mucho misterio.* He has no shadow. They say he has killed around sixty people."

Months later the retired judge told me, "*¡Cachama!* He was the one who could become invisible. One day the police cornered him, but he disappeared in a barrel of water. They were mystified until they saw bubbles emerging and were able to catch him."

The women walk away. The conversation is of little interest to them, and my novelty has worn off. Cachama belongs to a gang called Los Justicieros, "Those Who Wage Justice," dedicated to killing *rateros* living in the barrio and others who come in from other barrios. In other words, this is a gang undertaking its own *limpieza,* acting just like the *autodefensas,* only the "real" *autodefensas* are dedicated to killing the gangs! Maybe that's how it is all over the world now—an unstable hierarchy of gangs, some legal, others not.

How did Cachama become a gangster? He had a regular job and all of that but was robbed of his gold chain and badly beaten. He went back to work with one object in mind: get money; buy a gun; and exact revenge. Cachama is the name of a fish like a piranha. Oh! Yes! You would like to talk to Cachama all right, the man without a shadow. Then there was that other man who killed over 120 people until he himself was killed by other bandits at Navarro, the Cali garbage dump. He went down with tear gas and grenades, and then they ripped into him with bullets just to make sure.

V. hid out several months at Navarro. But under no conditions can you go there, he tells me when I express interest. You can only go if you're in with the *rosca*, the inner circle. Might makes right—he adds.

His brother has just finished four years in the Colombian army fighting the guerrilla and is now at home bored stiff and thinking of joining the *autodefensas*. V. has advised him to find a job with a security company instead (as if there's much difference).

He gets out of his chair to re-enact a fight he had with two guys on the cement bridge over the river here, long arms circling like a spider. I can see him balanced on the balustrade as I write these lines.

As I sit with V. feeding me these stories, I feel I've misunderstood the wild boys. He is so striking—skinny but muscular, lithe, with sloping shoulders and a long scar across his abdomen, clean-cut features, lovely smile, and basically so open and honest-seeming. (Yeah, he's a nice guy, says M., but a wild animal if you offend him or his woman.) Explanations of wayward youth assuming a sick personality, the evil of drugs, a deprived and depraved childhood, postmodern amorality, "the consumer society," the long-standing Colombian tradition of violence . . . all of that seems irrelevant and negative, aimed at explaining a deficit.

MAY 25

I WAKE AROUND FOUR IN THE MORNING staring at the silence.
My bag is packed, tickets ready. But I wake with this absolutely
clear and serene sense that I am not stepping onto a plane. I am
staying. And why do I keep coming back! Thirty years now! Do
I belong here? I think of youth out-of-control throughout the
world. It is beyond one's wildest imagination that kids could be
the cause of such widespread fear and revulsion as to bring a
town to its knees and thereby pave the way for paramilitaries.

No Robin Hood stuff with these gangs, stealing from the rich
and giving to the poor! Are you joking! J. and V. are absolutely
emphatic on this. I think of V.'s icy detachment. Well, not really
icy. But detachment, yes! And calm. Yes! That's what I'm looking for. The calmness in the violence, plus the mental power in
the concise, direct speech, with the voice as a decisive element in
the long-limbed body. Seemed like you could ask him anything,
he's so open. Transparent and unoffendable. At least with me. A
far cry from "the power of the powerless," that sneaky under-
hand mix of resentment and envy following hidden transcripts.

Quite contrary to all of that servant mentality, this is brazen, in-your-face, like the funerals in the cemetery, the wild clothes and haircuts, life in the fast lane like a shooting star. I get the feeling that whatever gangs mean, whatever the crazed armed fourteen-year-olds mean, it has to do with the self-assurance V. generates, the mix of self-assurance and bisexual erotic power that allows him to come across as totally honest. And surely just as it is this self-assurance that enabled him to leave the gangs, it is this erotic quality that enables gangsterhood.

M. had warned me, "But he's a wild animal if you offend his woman." And the young owner of a bar frequented by the gangs was scornful when I suggested unemployment or drugs as a cause for kids joining the gangs. "It's power they're after," he told me, "power to get girls. It's a sex thing. Women would flock to them—just as they now flock to the paras." In the village down the road a teenage mother I have known many years explained to me how, from a girl's point of view, having a gang member as a boyfriend was a source of protection for a girl as well as a source of prestige.

V. assures me there is no way the gangs could take on the paras—whom, with only a hint of irony, he calls "Power Rangers." The gangs are frightened. The paras are well equipped and can call on unlimited resources. As for my safety with the gangs, he laughs. "So long as you're not wearing gold rings or necklaces!"

But now Navarro has seduced me. A mountain of garbage! It beckons like the anti-Christ. Didn't V. himself say it was out of the question! And P. says, "You have to be tough as nails to keep what you find out there because people are going to stab you for it."

Stabbing is the image of violation I remember most vividly from those two weeks—the *chuzo*—same as the nightmare of having your front door stove in by paras with a crowbar. Always this sense of being opened and penetrated. How does being tough help you from being stabbed by those innumerable "others"? On the phone the judge tells me that small children fight with dogs for food out there at Navarro. But has she ever been there? I doubt it. "Navarro is where you learn," says P. Learn what?

Once someone found a bonanza there; 20 million pesos, or close to it. People find bags of money, gold rings, gold chains, and plastic bags full of false dollars.

"I can go on a garbage truck, I can go with M.," I say with bravado. I realize I don't mean it, but am trying to get myself psyched up. "No!" P. replies. "No way! That is their territory! They keep a sharp eye out for strangers. Has to be a *negro* from here." "It's a *republica independiente*," says M. "Only there are no passports."

Later in the morning I catch the bus into Cali and give a talk to history students at the university. It is fun. I am in another world and I am another person. The conversation is wide-ranging and continues over lunch, so different from the frenzied hurry of universities in the U.S. And here it seems like everything is decided collectively as we juggle our seating arrangements. It is beginning to rain. Shall we sit inside or out? What food to order?

Drinks? Then of course the pattern of talk, not one-on-one but a group affair. A student from a small town nearby explains that the *limpieza* there is complete and that the perpetrators have moved on. I tell her how things are where I am living. Her friend has just received a human rights bulletin that explains that the paras have changed tactics. Instead of massacres, they undertake "selective assassinations," and instead of rapid entry and exit, they remain. Suddenly my own experience gels. It becomes real. I have been validated by experts, in print.

After lunch I am taken to a supermarket near the university on the edge of the cane fields. With its lofty ceilings and spotless floors, it seems more like a cathedral. The food is displayed in bold fields of iridescent color, swathes of red, yellow, and green. Armed guards are everywhere. Fences surround fences like the stone walls the slaves built over two centuries to protect Cartagena from the pirates. My historian-guide tells me that her friends are too scared to go outside the city on the weekends for picnics, so they come here instead, even though they don't have money to buy anything.

I'm in a mess over Navarro, as big as the mess that is Navarro. It started when I came back from the university in the late afternoon and met M. excited about his idea of contacting Popó, whom people nickname "The Marshal," and who wields influence on both sides of the fence, with the law and with the underground. He has his criminal followers in Carlos Alfredo Díaz, and can be counted on to supply 200 votes in elections, for which service he gets contracts from the town worth up to 2 million pesos. M. thinks he would be just the person to arrange a field trip to Navarro.

I have a flash of insight as to whom the Marshal might be and question M. because when I first came here in late 1969, I was be-friended by the most charming man, Eusebio Popó, who rolled cigars for a living in his house at the end of town before the squatter settlement came into existence. Could the Marshal be his son? With a rush I recall a cute ten-year-old with the same high forehead and twinkling eyes as his father, dodging around his elbow with Eusebio barking in the middle of talking to me: "Re-spect! *¡Respéteme!*" I also remember that this cute-looking son was said years later to have kidnapped an elderly woman in Cali; he murdered either her or someone else who got in the way. And yet his father was such a delight, so clever and funny, and his mother always there looking after them all, especially her mother, who lay ill in bed complaining all the time. This was not your broken home, single-mother household scratching for a liv-ing. They were poor, but not as poor as a lot of people in town, and they were widely respected.

Popó comes in twitchy and snake-eyed, claiming to recognize me. M. had told him I thought I knew his father and mother, long since dead. He declines the invitation to sit, standing now on one leg, now on another, his body always at an angle, trying to de-ceive even the law of gravity. From the get-go I have a sinking feeling that he is preeminently the most untrustworthy person on the planet. He is so bad, he doesn't even bother to hide it. Or rather he has struck so many poses and plotted so many deceits that, in the maturity of his burned-out middle age, he can't keep

track of which identity he is meant to be other than protean becoming. We make plans for a visit to Navarro, which seems to
scare even him, and for once I think he is not lying. Rather, he
wants to use the danger to his advantage. We talk about his dad,
and he claps me on the back several times, calling me "family"
with great enthusiasm, smiling knowingly at M. as he does so. He
tells me he has to be honest and that he wants me to know he's
done time for murder. And also he has to be extremely careful
right now because of the *limpieza*. A door opens, and a sleepy-
eyed husband of one of the renters visiting from southern Cauca
walks out, trying to look as if he's not looking. But he has heard
everything, including our remarks about the paras. To whom is
he going to talk? I wonder. Popó explains to M. and me that he
has to talk with other thieves who know more than he does about
Navarro. After making and unmaking plans in a chaotic manner,
we eventually decide to meet tomorrow at 10:00 A.M. at a mutual
friend's place, next door to where Popó's parents lived. This
should give him time to gather three to four people to come to
talk about Navarro and prepare the visit, although he would pre-
fer not to visit on the weekend as the place then apparently goes
even crazier on alcohol and drugs. Popó indicates he would do
well to entertain his friends with some "sodas" tonight as a way
of encouraging them, but unfortunately has no money. . . . So I
give him the equivalent of five dollars. After all, we go back a
long way.

I find P. in the kitchen backed up against the stove, feet close
together, looking at the floor as if it is about to crack open. Never

has she spoken to me like this. We have completely misjudged the situation, she says. The paras are here in this town to kill the Marshal and the other gang leaders, and we have to be out-of-our-minds crazy to be even associating with him, let alone bringing him into her house in broad daylight. They stop at nothing. They come to your house anytime with crowbars and stomp in the door. M. looks as if he could die with shame. "She is right," he mumbles. *"¡Fue un error! ¡Fue un error!"* P. is on a rant. The whole terrible scene that is the *limpieza* swims before her eyes. Just yesterday, she says, two strange white guys were leaning against the wall of the Club Social scrutinizing everyone passing. Then they walked past her place, peering in the window. I feel terrible that I've pulled her into this mess as if it were all along a game.

We agree on a plan to (try to) get rid of the Marshal and P. will find the high school student who helps her out on occasions to see if he will act as a guide to Navarro. M. leaves, and on a stool on the pavement the other side of the street I see the renter's husband sipping a beer staring at us as I close the front door with a bang. In the meantime I go stir-crazy rereading the daily newspaper that M. has brought me, as I don't want to walk outside because I feel marked, and P. has been chastising me for being conspicuous. Forty-five minutes later she returns with a black kid. It turns out the kid does not know Navarro, but his brother has told him it is extremely dangerous. However, his dad, a peasant farmer, goes every week out there to see what valuable garbage he can find. The kid was stopped by the paras in the street a week or so back as he was running away from them. They asked him his name and consulted their list (at which point in his story the kid extends his arm fully to show how long the list was). They told him never to run away from them again.

M. returns with a heavy-set, serious-looking, man from the Patía valley who, last year, took me to the airport in his taxi and for seven years worked in proximity to Navarro as the overseer of a gang of over one hundred sugarcane workers. He is the cousin of a family whom I lived next door to for several months in the late 1970s. He explains Navarro to me. It is an artificial mountain. The concept is hard to grasp. I had seen it way in the distance several years ago from the window of the bus traveling to and from Cali and wondered how strange it looked, rising abruptly out of the valley floor. It never occurred to me it was artificial, and certainly not that it was made of garbage. Instead, it made me daydream about the Indians who lived there before the Spanish Conquest in the valley of Lili, as described by Cieza de León mid-sixteenth century. I would imagine Cieza and his boys dropping by for a little chat with the Indians by the banks of the river, trying not to look too curious about the gold rings through the noses of their hosts. In those far-off days, so it is recorded, the valley was full of swamps and reeds, fish and fowl, with monkeys screeching in tall trees.

After working in the cane fields around Navarro as a labor overseer, the taxi driver drove an eighteen-wheel oil tanker all over Colombia for three years. This is a man you can trust to handle any situation, like most people I have met from the Patía valley, the hottest place outside of hell in our universe. The pay was excellent, the work dangerous, and he made money sufficient to buy this taxi and build a house that he now wants to fill with porcelain panthers, just as bandit-chief Nemecio did.

He describes the awful smell and the buzzards out at Navarro. If you look offended and hold your nose, you run the risk of being killed, he tells me with a knowing look. There are about 800 people digging in garbage there, and they find bags of gold chains and money, he assures me.

Navarro is shaped like a cone-shaped seashell, but with a flattened top instead of a point. Round and round in ever diminishing circles, the garbage trucks ascend. When they reach the top, they unload. Earth is brought in to layer the garbage, and there is a chimney to allow the gases underneath to escape. Concrete channels leading to the once beautiful Lili River carry away nameless fluids. Navarro is awfully dangerous, concludes the taxi driver, slowly shaking his head—at which point, trusting him completely, I give up there and then on the idea of going.

MAY 26

UNUSUALLY COLD AND GRAY MORNING. I stay in bed under my mosquito net, where I feel all the more like a prince when P., having cooked breakfast for the renters, brings me a cup of milkless sugared coffee with a *pan de horno,* a doughnut-shaped crisp bread with some cheese in the dough. What luxury. Radio news. Bulbous green and yellow plantain leaves wave at me through the barred window. Surprised I could sleep after Popó. I keep turning over the idea of a visit to Navarro. Maybe I could get away with it after all?

Funny thing, fieldwork; how people lay treasure before you but you don't see it. This is what happened with Navarro. The lawyer had mentioned it to me when describing what he saw as the security threat posed by the barrio Carlos Alfredo Díaz, connected to Navarro by an underground circuit of drugs and weapons traveling by lost paths winding through the sugarcane that, when mature, is close to twelve feet high. People who are not used to cane tell stories about getting lost and dying in cane-fields. In *North by Northwest*, Alfred Hitchcock evoked some of that when he had Cary Grant try to evade a crop-dusting airplane by hiding in a corn field. Sugarcane is even denser and higher.

There was another detail the lawyer gnawed upon, like a dog with a bone. Because so many of the homes in CAD are unfinished, the backyards communicate with one another so that if the police make a raid, the inhabitants can whip out the back and be down the end of the street long before the police realize what's happening. This didn't seem that important to me. I chalked it up to paranoia and the way he would obsessively fuss over some intricate detail as a way of avoiding panic. But now I see this image as one marked out, like Navarro itself, in striking architectural terms. Navarro is the monument. CAD is the labyrinth. The two are destined to converge.

Pulling aside the curtain that is my door, P. leans against the wall as I lie in bed, and we talk about everything and nothing. Our mornings often begin like this, a time when the soul opens out in a strange comfort zone where the brute facts of life and the delicacy of personal invention come together. Monument and labyrinth. She is a political philosopher, and I am her scribe yet also the outsider upon whom you try out ideas, dispel dogmas, and give voice to rarely voiced fears. Like dreamwork we mull over the refuse of the previous day in the *telenovela* that is Colombia. Even though the U.S. has defined the paras as terrorists and claims it will deny them and their supporters visas, she believes the paras are so deeply entrenched in the police, the army, and the rich, so intertwined in so many ways, that such interventions by the U.S. will have little effect. What are the men who finish their military service going to do for a job but join the paras? she asks. A friend who works as a cook for the batallion in Cali tells her many of the officers are paras or closely connected with them. As for the state prosecutors here, they must be relieved, even pleased, the paras are here. If they were doing their job properly, wouldn't they be *amenazada* ("threatened")? Wouldn't they have fled? How come the paras drive brazenly around killing people in the daylight with tons of witnesses and nobody does anything? A judge was able to check the death list to see what danger he was in. Doesn't that prove a tight relation between the paras and the state? The judge said there are schoolteachers on the list as well as *delincuentes.*

P. now thinks the paras are here to protect the recently created tax-free "industrial park." Castaño, the leader of the paras, was here a few weeks back, she says, and the town has been selected to be a fortress in their plan to take over the entire region. . . . Free thought. Free fall. She thinks the guerrilla and the paras cede territories to each other as much as they fight over them, that they are dividing up the country between themselves.

Although Popó has been told via a cousin that we have to postpone our thieves' gathering ("because I have an appointment with the embassy," M. said! What an imagination!), he turns up at 9:00 in the morning just as the taxi pulls up. This is what I had been dreading. *"Mucho cuidado con Popó,"* mutters the taxi driver under his breath as he polishes an invisible speck on the bonnet of his cab. Popó approaches me, saying he met with his gangster friends last night on my behalf but had to pawn his watch to ensure they had enough to drink and get in the right mood. Could I give him the money he needs to get his watch back? "No!" I reply, surprised at myself. He twitches his snake eyes and walks away, if walk it be. But P. is terrified he'll be back. "They are like sorcerers," she says, "they are so clever at spinning their webs and drawing you in. Kidnapping is what he's got in mind right now." Lesson for the day: You thought it was all about violence, guns and knives, grenades and mortars. How wrong you are. It's sorcery that you should be scared of, clever people manipulating situations, stimulating desire, taking advantage of insecurities, guilt, envy, and misunderstandings. I settle back as in the driver's capable hands the cab sets off to Navarro with the radio providing the latest news on the two bomb attacks in Bogotá that morning. A colonel advises us not to get too absorbed in our thoughts as we go to work, but to be alert for strange activities—as if we aren't, dear Colonel, every moment of the day—and second, don't loiter but go straight to work. The president comes on next with telephone numbers for the citizenry to call if they see anything suspicious. He says he wants every citizen to become the eyes and ears of the state. A pedestrian is interviewed, too. Voice of the people: *Los buenos son muchos, los malos son pocos, y tenemos que acabar con esa gente.* ("The good guys are many, the bad guys are few, and we've got to finish off this scum.")

The taxi driver gets nervous as we swing onto the dirt road leading to Navarro. His plan had been to stop at the last row of houses, the last sign of civilization you might say, talk to people and suss out the situation, but instead, he keeps going. It's been raining. The sky is gloomy. The road is enclosed by high scrub like a tunnel. Our smart little yellow taxi designed for city streets sends out a bow wave of finely churned mud. Sometimes through the trees on the north side of the road we see a row of gray cement homes two stories high with ornate iron bars protecting them. They look like prisons. Or birdcages. I shudder at the thought of living in one, under the spell of Navarro. Everything seems covered with slime and a putrid smell. Meanwhile the driver is telling me and M. and nobody in particular that Colombia is full of *gente mala*. "Bad people." He pauses. *Muy mala,* he emphasizes. I think back to Popó. He is inside me now, doing his sorcery, just like P. said he would. I think I've got a bead on him because his dad and I were such friends, but I know that in some awful way that can work against me, too. I will be sentimental and too trusting.

Most of all, however, as I sit in the back of the cab on our suicide mission slithering over the mud, I think of the ex-bandit V., in contrast to Popó, as two sides of a coin; V. showing off his knife-fighting skills, re-enacting the fight on the bridge over the river with such flair and making me think how much of banditry is devoted to flair, to living as a knife-fighter on a bridge facing up to two attackers, his long arms weaving their web like a spider. Could those arms be more than a match for Popó's sorcery spinning you into his web? Why did fate select two such different figures for me? A violent ex-gangster, the epitome of honesty with his body of calm at the center of the storm. The other, twice his age, a shaking morass of criminal deceit with the magic of a sorcerer inserting himself into you like the paras with their crowbars or the proverbial Chinese painter who disappears into his own painting. Perhaps it goes like this: the young gangsters get killed, but people like Popó, the Marshal, are timeless.

Every now and again a garbage truck comes toward us like a tank beating through the mud. Our driver stops one and asks if it's okay to proceed. It is comforting to find here another human being whose relation to garbage is distinctly normal, dedicated to throwing it away and maintaining boundaries as they should be maintained. Working for the state, what's more. Nice, cheery chaps, they tell us it's okay to proceed. We go on and see the silhouette of a small group of people resting in the lower limbs of a tree. The driver slows down, gives them the thumbs-up sign, and speeds on, not wanting to stop and let them get close. I find it unnerving that he seems to fear even these pathetic figures. A dead horse with a swollen belly lies on the road. Further on, an aged couple are feverishly stuffing things into a bag by the side of a torn and rain-sodden mustard-colored sofa upended on the bank. They cast a furtive glance but keep at what they are doing. Why so furtive? It's not as if they are robbing a bank. I wonder how the taxi can keep going in this slush, neither water nor mud, and whether we could turn around if accosted.

The driver swerves to the right and stops abruptly at a turn-off to a concrete bridge with guardrails on which a row of buzzards are perched. They flap lazily a few feet away as we get out of the car. They are not frightened. You're the one who should be frightened.

We walk onto the bridge. There is a huge concrete drain running twenty feet beneath us, more like ravine. Perfectly straight, it disappears into the horizon of the sugarcane fields. As far as the eye can see there are black pipes maybe a foot in diameter crossing the drain every fifty feet or so, the same height as the bridge. Every pipe has buzzards on it. At times the liquids running through the drain must rise as high as these pipes because, along with the buzzards, rags and garbage hang down from each one. The lush grasses sprouting from either side seem more blue than green, mutants fed by swirling toxins. A four-wheel-drive car comes across the bridge with a sour-looking plantation foreman and disappears into the cane fields. Looking along this river of pestilence with rags and the buzzards hanging over it, I get the feeling that Colombia's problems are far greater than guerrilla, paras, or drugs.

We get back into our little yellow car and drive on for a few minutes. The mountain rears into sight. "Tower of Babel," mutters M., never lost for a biblical quotation. It is a chalk-gray pyramid with spiraling ribs. Like insects, trucks circle their way along the ribs to the top. Hanging over it all is a spotted haze which, on closer inspection, turns out to be a cloud of buzzards. The smell is what I imagine dead bodies would smell like after a week or two in the sun and rain. As we get closer you see buzzards lined up like beads on the rings around the mountain that give it its shell-like form. It could be jewelry.

With bulky clothes covering them entirely, two young women, their hair in shower caps, are picking their way into a heap of garbage by the side of the road. One wears gloves. We try to talk with them, but they turn away without a word. I have heard that you can make a better living here than in most jobs, with the exception of *la vida facil,* meaning drugs, which is probably even more dangerous.

We reach the foot of the mountain. There are two sturdy metal gates, a weigh-station, and a guard-box on either side of the gates, with three trigger-happy guards, shotguns at the ready. They won't let us in, about which I am much relieved, and they won't allow photographs. Our driver backs the car to one side, ready for a quick getaway. In the guard box by a narrow pedestrian entrance there is a woman in uniform watching people file in and out. There are handwritten signs on the glass: PEOPLE UNDER 14 NOT ALLOWED and HAVE GOOD DAY. Trucks with garbage come every few minutes. Sometimes they have one or two people clinging to the back of the truck who will claim the entire load for themselves. There are many women and young people under fourteen years of age. Every day there are dead people found here, the driver says.

Three bulldozers spread the garbage, maintaining the cone shape of the mountain with its circular ridges. You can make out people swarming behind the garbage trucks like birds darting on seed in a freshly sown field. We can distinguish dark tents on the top, where people live. The mountain is about 180 feet high, with trees and grass growing up to about a quarter of the way. It is an ecologically attuned garbage dump designed by a Spanish company so that the garbage slowly sinks with its layers of dirt to compost and eventually become earth. One day this might even revert to sugarcane, our driver tells me. Who knows? The possibilities are endless. Maybe one day even the sugarcane may become garbage and revert to the woods and swamps that were this beautiful valley, once a lake onto which floated ash from the volcanoes.

The ash settled to the bottom of the lake. The lake drained to form the Cauca River, which meanders hundreds of miles north to the Caribbean. The bed of the lake dried out to become the valley composed of swamps and rich black topsoil up to fifteen feet deep, making it a cornucopia of plant life 125 miles long and 30 miles wide. "The Eden of the Americas," Simón Bolívar is supposed to have said on seeing it in the early nineteenth century. But the native forests have gone, as have the artificial forests created by the freed slaves. At first the sugar was hungry for labor, but then chemicals and machines made the workers idle. The slum towns festered. The second decisive event is cocaine, and the third is the kids. They are not anything like the generations before. Like the plants that went under, like the forest that disappeared, human nature as much as nature is now facing a brave new world for which there is no history or prehistory, other than this mountain shaped like a seashell.

MAY 27

RAIN FALLING EARLY MORNING. P. at the curtain. We sip our coffee. "Politics is a drug," she says angrily, out of the blue. *La política* is the term she uses. Sounds grander than just saying "politics." *La política* suggests a character in a baroque-era play, a character like the Ogre who is also the Seducer. Tarot cards. You can see them strut by. *La política*. What does it mean? Here's what I think, me the note-taker and note-maker. *La política* means Navarro reaching for the sky, where heaven and hell fuse so as to invigorate each other through the putrefying medium of death—dead bodies, dead horses, dead sofas, the glint of cocaine and gold in the form of rings and neck-chains lost in dirty plastic bags along with shapeless shoes. This is the drug we take daily, this is *la política* as when P. asserts that eight out of ten people in this town are glad the paras are here assassinating wild youth. This is *la política,* where Popó gets 2-million-peso contracts for supplying 200 votes, where the factories rising up out of the good earth of the prehistoric valley floor cut deals with the town's administration, and then with the paras. Everyone knows the only way to get ahead is to get a public position so you can be bribed—meaning drugged—and drugged far more deeply than with cocaine, drugged with Navarro's seeping fluids turning the green grass blue as the buzzards hop like arthritic ballet dancers. And of course this is only the first circle, the first circle of Navarro. There are twelve more to go, real and imaginary, laced with stories like buzzards, such as the officers in the Colombian army selling not only arms but also their own soldiers as kidnap victims to the guerrilla; or the fact that the medical doctors' association of the valley is right there behind the paras, along with the cattlemen and the industrialists—and now the poor of the slum towns are cheering them on as well. The paras or *autodefensas,* *pistoleros* or "the people walking around"—whatever name you wish to use—they are also merely in the first circle, hopping along with their lists, I.D. numbers, and photographs, lists as long as a small boy's extended arm, lists compiled, so it is said, from police and army intelligence, lists as long as a small boy's arm, but getting shorter by the day.

Late afternoon. L.'s daughter, running breathless around the corner of the girl's school, tells me her twenty-eight-year-old cousin who worked as a clerk for the municipal government has just been shot dead by her separated husband who then shot himself dead as well. Later I hear he had two other women. One fled to Spain, and the other had her face broken open by him last week—so L. tells me, back to her old form once more. *"Un tipo muy patán,"* she adds, from *pata* meaning "foot"; *patán,* meaning like a horse that kicks out wildly.

As I approach the wake through silent dark streets there are cars blocking the road. A tent extends from the house out onto the street, with some fifty chairs underneath. I see a few people I know and go in the side entrance to the patio full of women sitting one next to the other. I greet the mother, stock-still in shock, and go into the main room, open to the street, where the coffin is placed at hip level so one can see the face of the dead woman. L. presents me to the grandmother, who is delighted to see me, cracking into a broad smile. It was she who had taken me out to the cane fields years ago with the cooks who set up their fires in the fields and told me about the devil contracts some of the cane workers were said to make to boost their production. I wander outside where people talk in small groups or are sitting still. An elegant older man with upright carriage and silver hair asks if I remember him. I say I do, but it takes me a while, back twenty-four years to Don René, who had a small general store right on the corner of the second-last street of town, opposite where Popó lived. I remember how barefoot kids would go in there in noisy gangs and steal rice from the open bags on the floor by lifting their shirts at the waist to make big pockets. Rice, "the sacred pearl," they used to call it. Now it's more than rice they're after. He straightaway gets into what P. calls the "golden age" story about how great things were here before the sugar plantations, and the old men either side of him add to his recollections, nodding enthusiastically, me included. It is as much a politeness to me, the author and historian, as it is nostalgia. A middle-aged man with bulging eyes and the stamp of a politician takes me aside and tell me how he has an appointment with the Canadian embassy and is sure he will be granted political asylum there for himself and his family.

All the conversations are about something other than the immediate cause of our congregating, but are pervaded by it. L. stands at the foot of the coffin fingering the white beads of her rosary. Other women join her. They pray. They chant. They sing. They stand like tree trunks, their dignity overwhelming, their clothes threadbare.

Walter Benjamin has a passage on the rosary in what is probably his most famous essay, "Theses on the Philosophy of History," which he wrote in 1940 shortly before he killed himself on the Spanish-French border, fleeing that other paramilitary organization, the Gestapo. Written in staccato style in a series of loosely connected yet hard-hitting paragraphs, any one of which could be chiseled onto a gravestone, it argues for a mode of writing in which the historian "stops telling the sequence of events like the beads of a rosary. Instead, he grasps the constellation which his own era has formed with a definite earlier one. Thus he establishes a conception of the present as 'the time of the now' which is shot through with chips of messianic time."[18]

That sums up the method of this chronicle which I now bring to an end. It was not a method I consciously sought. It followed the paths of recollection and their unexpected associations through different lapses of time as they opened out from a diary I kept for two weeks in May 2001. The "now time" that Benjamin refers us to is incandescent for me in a continuous present the diarist puts onto the page as events slip away the instant they are recorded, yet in doing so they trigger recollections with other events long past so as to create meaningful constellations, more meaningful in that, as Benjamin points out, they connect the present era with an earlier one through unexpected juxtaposition.

Yet can this be as sharply contrasted with the rosary as Benjamin makes out? The rosary is what I will always remember passing through L.'s hands as she faces the coffin chanting and singing with her beautiful voice, leading the other woman no less steady on their feet. Actually the rosary is less a narrative order than a response to events, just as the diary is. With its repetition and its rhythms, the rosary offers space for meditation. The rosary provides images to think through unspeakable events that, because of their power and their gravity, blast aside contexts and schemes of interpretation, leaving nothing but the event, just that, glowing silence of the unique filled with the chants the rosary feeds through one's fingers. And if the rosary is by definition repetitive, it at least provides the steadiness of ritual in the space of death, whose chips of messianic time remain violently silent in my chronicle.

POSTSCRIPT, NEW YORK

February 22, 2002

A friend dropped by. He has lived in New York thirty years but was born in the town my diary concerns. He has just returned from a two-week visit there. He tells me everything has changed since he was there a year ago. Now you can walk safely in the streets, day or night. The market which before was practically empty is full of people and goods. His mother doesn't have to bend over protecting her money when she makes a purchase. He points out that in areas under their control, the guerrilla carry out *limpiezas*, too. He tells me that a middle-aged friend of his was killed by the paras shortly before his arrival. Someone to whom he owed fifty dollars went to the paras asking them to collect the debt in exchange for half of it. The paras knocked on the friend's door. He told them they were out of line. They argued. And he was shot dead. My New York friend adds that he has never seen the cemetery so full of flowers. This very day I read that in the eighteen months under Ariel Sharon's rule, some 1,300 Palestinians and Israelis have been killed. We think of Israel as bloody siege, and our heart stops in our mouth. Meanwhile, in a small Colombian town of 50,000 people, quietly and unnoticed by the world at large, some 300 people have been assassinated since the paras arrived exactly one year ago.

July 2002

I myself returned seventeen months after the arrival of the paras, fourteen months after the events recorded in my diary. The paras were killing two to three "delinquents" a week. Some people suspect many murders are actually carried out by the army's intelligence service as well. However most assassinations are done *en frente*—openly in public view—while the police and army kill you from behind, *a espaldas,* and out of town. Nobody dares protest. At the most, people just whisper to one another at the funerals for the victims. Vandalism has disappeared; there is no breaking of windows or smashing of signs, the kids who make a living pushing carts to and from the market no longer fight among themselves, and there are no disputes in the streets. At a meeting with parents, the school principal refused to resign. Some paras arrived. *¿Te vas o te quedas?* "Are you staying or leaving?" He picked up his papers and left. And there are no more strikes by workers. Despite the apparent safety, people are nervous. I had to be escorted at night. The paras have subcontracted some of their security operations to gang members who have joined them. The central plaza was full of smart new yellow taxis with two-way radios. The drivers make two to three trips a day to the Cali airport for businessmen and engineers traveling to the new factories in the tax-free industrial park. There are two ATM machines in the plaza as well. On asking M. once again how safe I am, he replies, "Of course you're safe. In fact they'll protect you!" To which P. replies in disbelief: "You believe in them? They are assassins. I could never trust an assassin." Nevertheless, she now sometimes leaves the front door open during the day, something I have never once seen in thirty years. The *limpieza* is over. The *limpieza* was a success.

Till the next time.

A VIEW FROM THE OUTSIDE

SOMEWHERE, Isaac Deutscher distinguishes between the portrait and the X ray as different forms of social commentary. Each has its legitimate function, each its weaknesses, and to some degree the two forms complement one another. As a portrait, my diary presents events from the inside, as it were. It thereby establishes a human continuity, tied to the intimate details of the passing of the days, as well as to a wavering degree of self-consciousness about the art of writing—what Norman Mailer calls "the spooky art." But in closing this diary, I thought it necessary to present an outside view, an X ray, as it were, that the reader might find useful as a form of orientation to the current violence in Colombia.

At the outset, let me picture Colombia physically, a nation now of 43 million people living close to the equator with little seasonal variation but great variation in climate and vegetation by height above sea level. Three chains of cloud-covered mountains and largely extinct volcanoes run the length of the country, north to south. To be in Colombia is to have your body think three-dimensionally—cold country, hot country, and temperate, with all manner of difference thus manifest, cultural as well as physical. A lush and fertile country bounded by two oceans, the Pacific and the Caribbean, with spectacular landscapes and an extraordinary diversity of plant life, its people live for the most part in a handful of cities such as Bogotá, the capital, population approximately 6 million, and somewhat smaller cities such as Medellín, Cali, and Barranquilla. Unlike other Latin American countries, Colombia's population is not concentrated in one megalopolis, and this in turn reflects the radical decentralization of the country with its strong regional subcultures and fractured government.

At the time of the Spanish conquest around 1500, the people indigenous to what is now called Colombia existed in many small chiefdoms. Unlike the Inca empire, which came as far north as Colombia's southern border at Pasto, such small-scale chiefdoms were difficult for the Spaniards to control, so they bought African slaves from Dutch, British, and French slavers to work the gold mines, Colombia being the chief source of gold in the Spanish empire. Today, Colombia has black majorities in the forests of the isolated Pacific coast, the urbanized and densely populated Caribbean coast, and at the south of the Cauca valley, to name the most important areas, blacks forming around 10 percent of the national population. Pockets of indigenous people, preserving language and, in some cases, distinctive clothing, predominate in the Amazon, the Guajira peninsula, the Sierra Nevada de Santa Marta on the Caribbean coast, as well as in the central mountains—the Cordillera Central del Cauca—where they have been absolutely crucial in making Indian ethnic identity a powerful political force since the 1970s—despite the fact that indigenous people amount to no more than 1 percent of the population.

If gold was the principal export of the colony—which came to an end in the early nineteenth century with the Wars of Independence—then cocaine is the principal export of the past twenty years, although oil is also important and getting more so, with President George W. Bush sending in U.S. troops to guard the pipelines. This pretty well sums up our age, I suppose, cocaine and oil, both surrounded by soldiers bristling with guns. Oh my! What a world!

Cocaine burst onto the scene around 1980 with the eclipse of an older Colombia that had been more rural than urban and in which two feuding political parties, Liberals and Conservatives, had administered the country for over a century. The lethal War of the Thousand Days ended with the Conservative Party victorious in 1901. The hegemony of that party continued for another thirty years, the last decade of which saw land invasions by peasants and strikes against *yanqui* imperialism—the 1924 strike against the U.S. Tropical Oil Company, and the 1928 strike against the United Fruit Company by banana workers, which resulted in their being massacred by the Colombian army, described by Gabriel García Márquez in *One Hundred Years of Solitude*. The same decade saw the spread of Socialist ideas and the formation of the Colombian Communist Party—all of which testified to a groundswell of unease throughout much of the country that led to the electoral defeat of the Conservatives in 1930. With the return to power of the Conservative Party in 1946, in its virulently Fascist phase, the scene was set for an apocalyptic struggle known as *La Violencia* between the two parties, following the assassination of the charismatic Liberal Party leader Jorge Eliécer Gaitán on the streets of Bogota in 1948.

At first *La Violencia* took the form of a fratricidal bloodletting between the two parties which, even though not all that different ideologically, had long resembled mutually hostile religions, so powerful were the sentiments each could arouse, membership being something you inherited along with your mother's milk. But with the Conservatives in control of the state, *La Violencia* created new forms of armed resisitance that emerged organically from groups of Liberal Party peasants trying to protect themselves. Thus was born in 1966 the Moscow-oriented guerrilla now known as the FARC, today the oldest and largest guerrilla group in the world, with some estimated 18,000 combatants. Other guerrilla organizations were created around the same time, notably the Cuba-oriented, priest-led ELN, founded in 1965, currently about 5,000 strong. Notable, too, was the more populist, more urban, and more media-conscious M-19 guerrilla, with many university students and intellectuals in its leadership. Founded in 1970 as a more lively, less doctrinaire version of the peasant-based FARC, the M-19 pulled off some spectacular stunts, such as the takeover of the Dominican embassy with a party of ambassadors in full swing in 1980, and the disastrous occupation of the National Palace of Justice in 1985, which was stormed by the army, leaving eleven supreme court justices dead and all but one of the guerrilla.

With the example and sometimes the support of the Cuban revolution (1959), the late sixties and seventies witnessed something like a boom period for guerrilla struggle throughout much of Latin America, along with the celebrated literary "boom" in magical realism, proving, if proof be needed, that history works in strange ways. There was Che Guevara's group in Bolivia, Douglas Bravo in Venezuela, the *montoneros* in Argentina, and the dashing Tupamaros of Uruguay, as well as groups in Peru, peaking with the huge mobilization under the Sendero Luminoso in the 1980s. In Brazil there was an innovation with short-lived urban guerrillas in the 1960s, and in Guatemala a left-wing guerrilla had formed by 1963. All in all an incredible ferment and an incredible period in Latin American and indeed in world history, all ending in monstrous failure, monstrous oppression, and in most cases monstrous military dictatorships replacing more open governments.

But in Colombia things were different, and have stayed different. Guerrilla warfare continues and the government finds itself bogged down in a military stalemate. The army is small compared with other Latin American armies, much smaller than what many counter-insurgency experts say is required. As for the significance of U.S. military aid, the eighty-plus helicopters provided so far by Plan Colombia are insignificant considering the number needed to wage such a war, as seen in El Salvador in the

Reagan era. Current wisdom has it that this relative weakness forces the Colombian army to support a semi-secret terror apparatus. But this argument forgets that in El Salvador, which had a huge army and massive U.S. support, the government's defense forces fomented and tolerated quite extraordinary levels of torture and rape, death squads, and other human rights abuses. In other words, more U.S. military aid for Colombia does not necessarily mean fewer human rights violations. This is especially worrying given that after September 11, it would seem that the vigilance of the U.S. Congress in monitoring human rights, in Colombia and elsewhere, is much diminished, and dangerously so, because there can be no guarantee that the army's support of the paramilitaries will decline—it will merely become more subtle, more indirect, and more secretive—and there is no guarantee that corruption within the army and the police will not divert the aid.

Current wisdom also maintains that the FARC has lost sight of its earlier, utopian Socialist objectives. Instead, the FARC has become increasingly militaristic in focus, paying for its recruits and armaments by heavy involvement in the drug trade, kidnapping, and extortion—to the extent that many previous sympathizers now accuse it of being purely a criminal organization led by "dinosaur Marxists" with a taste for *Rambo*-style violence. But one should be careful not to confuse means with ends and thereby dismiss the possibility that the FARC's long-term goal remains creating a far more equal, and in many ways a far better, society than at present exists. This is not to say that such an outcome, if achieved by the FARC, would not also be painfully authoritarian.

But far too much attention is spent on the headline-grabbing drama of the state versus the guerrilla. For the more fundamental issue in many ways is the sordid everyday one of grinding poverty, street crime, and the nightmare life of kids. During the 1980s, murder due to nonpolitical street crime started to soar, and today murder in the streets remains far higher than figures for deaths occurring in armed conflict between the guerrilla and the state's armed forces. Such street crime, as I call it, more often than not involves young men and women from poor families who became a profound enigma to their parents no less than to the authorities. A new world had dawned with regard to music, dress, haircuts, sexuality, dance, drugs, glue sniffing, child prostitution, weapons, language, and an unwillingness to work or accept authority as their more docile-seeming parents did. This worldwide phenomenon was greatly exacerbated in Colombia with the rise of *la vida facil*, or "the easy life," opened up by drug trafficking. A whole new political and cultural economy was fashioned out of prohibition and its transgression.

For the root of the "drug problem" lies not with the people who take drugs nor with those who traffic in them. Instead, it lies in the inevitable effects of prohibition. It is prohibition that makes drugs valuable and the trade violent. So long as prohibition of drugs is maintained in the U.S. and elsewhere, it is extremely unlikely there will be peace in Colombia.

Meanwhile, the U.S. government pursues policies that seem designed to keep drug profits high. Instead of legalizing drugs, diminishing jail sentences for drug dealers, and tackling demand inside the U.S. with medical aid for addicts, the resources are diverted to spraying coca and poppy fields in Colombia and mounting bullying attempts at interdiction. Since 1980, the U.S. has spent more than $150 billion in its "War Against Drugs" and civil liberties in the U.S. have been eroded as part of that war. Spraying herbicides poisons the Colombian forest, the rivers, and peasant crops, and so far has done nothing but lead to an expansion of the acreage under cultivation. By combining this aerial onslaught of poison with military support for attacks on the guerrilla, attacks now sanctioned by the U.S. Congress, which had until recently been reluctant to see the U.S. dragged into a guerrilla war, the violence in Colombia is exacerbated. It remains to be seen if the Colombian military will attack the paramilitaries with anything like the vigor it attacks the guerrilla, even though the paramilitaries are now also designated "terrorists" by the U.S. State Department.

As for the paramilitaries, it should be obvious from my diary just how complicated is their history and organization. Undoubtedly they have roots going far back to the ways people, rich or poor, would create their own police forces to protect their towns, their farms, or their haciendas. In my diary, I note the formation of such police by large landowners in the Cauca valley in the 1930s, but the phenomenon must be more general and far older than that. To follow the threads into more recent times, we can point to the *chulavitas* and *pájaros* that were included in the state's police forces during *La Violencia* with devastating results, and then to the way the Colombian army in the 1960s as part of its counter-guerrilla strategy copied the self-defense organizations that peasants established during *La Violencia* so as to protect themselves from the *chulavitas* and the army. A tremendous boost to paramilitarization was provided in the 1980s by the drug cartels, especially those of Medellín, whose immensely wealthy bosses and lieutenants, in their grandiose attempts to emulate the aristocracy, acquired huge tracts of cattle land in the center of the country in the blastingly hot Magdalena valley. This area had long been subject to the FARC demanding protection money—the *vacuna* or *boleteo*—as part of its struggle, in the words of one cattleman, "to combat petty crime and create equality by fighting the rich and the exploiters."[19] Greatly irked by this, and by kidnapping, the new landowners channeled money into the stridently anti-Communist self-defense organization that cattlemen, together with the national army and local businessmen, had set up in 1982 around the Texas Petroleum Company base at Puerto Boyacá on the Magdalena River. There was a huge billboard at the entrance to the town that sent chills down my spine when I saw it in 1989: WELCOME TO THE ANTI-COMMUNIST CAPITAL OF COLOMBIA. This self-defense group had a large, even national, reach, sending its assassins as far afield as the bloodsoaked fields of the banana plantations of Urabá near Panama, to the north, and to the coca fields of the Putumayo, at the headwaters of the Amazon, to the south. A sophisticated organization, it provided health services, locally, and pensions for the widows of any of its members killed in action.

The further nationalization of the paramilitaries under the umbrella of the AUC (the United Self-Defense Groups of Colombia), was provided by the agile Carlos Castaño. Listening to him, you sense a holy crusade, yet as Alfredo Rangel points out: "The notorious frequency with which the paras situate themselves wherever drug dealers are active—or where there are mega-projects such as hydroelectic dams or new highways pushing up land values—indicates that behind paramilitarism there is something other than an altruistic interest in counterinsurgency."[20] One only has to think of the "industrial parks" established close to the town in my diary to get his point. But this "something other" is a lot more than money. It is also fear of "delinquency," of the squatters at the end of town, and of the putrefying mass that is Navarro—a fear that cherishes violence for its own sake, alone.

2001—The Year of the Diary

In 2001, more than 4,000 people were victims of political killings, and some 300,000 were displaced, bringing the total of displaced persons to 2 million (in a total population of 43 million). The large numbers of persons kidnapped, including children, makes Colombia the most kidnap-prone society in the world. According to Amnesty International, torture and mutilation of cadavers remained widespread during 2001, particularly by paramilitary groups. Moreover, "new evidence emerged of continuing collusion between the armed forces and illegal paramilitary groups." Indeed, such collusion has strengthened, while "impunity for human rights abuses remained the norm."[21]

By 2001, the situation was not only ghastly, but getting worse. Eleven human rights defenders and nine journalists were murdered. A dozen more journalists were forced into exile. Seven Colombian government investigators and one judge investigating paramilitaries were murdered. And despite jaw-dropping paramilitary violence, the then-president of Colombia had failed to take effective action to break the connection between the paramilitaries and the armed forces. Even though the armed forces continued to be implicated in human rights violations—a point neatly overlooked by the U.S. State Department that has certified to the contrary—"the vast majority of abuses are committed by paramilitary groups (in some cases in cooperation with governmental troops) and to a lesser extent by guerrillas."[22] In the first ten months of 2001, ninety-two massacres were reported, such as the paramilitary massacre—described as "typical"—that occurred on January 17, 2001, in a village called Chengue in the north of Colombia. Some fifty paras pulled dozens of people from their homes and assembled them in two groups. One by one the paras killed twenty-four of them by crushing their heads with heavy stones and a sledgehammer. As the paras left, they set fire to the village. According to a *Washington Post* reporter who visited within hours of the attack and interviewed more than two dozen survivors, the Colombian military helped coordinate the massacre by providing safe passage for the paras, while holding a mock daylong battle that sealed off the area to anyone else and allowed the paras time to identify their victims and kill them.[23] Be it noted that by June 2002, the paras' umbrella organization, the

AUC, claims to have filled one third of the seats in the Colombian Congress with its sympathizers in its ongoing efforts to gain status and legitimacy in peace negotiations.[24]

Strange things are afoot in the latest developments as of 2003. The new president, long in favor of paramilitaries, whom he himself boosted when governor of the state of Antioquia, has now to deal with the U.S. State Department labelling them "terrorists." For the first time ever there have been occasional reports of armed clashes between the national army and paramilitaries, coinciding with battles between paramilitaries themselves.

But as usual, the name of the game is confusion, partly deliberate, partly not; and as with the U.S. government since September 11 in its war against terrorism, events prove that there is something insufferably attractive about the margin of law where the state re-creates the very terror it is meant to combat, such that there will always be not only a military, but a paramilitary as well.

NOTES

1. Jean Genet. *Prisoner of Love* (Hanover, NH: University Press of New England/Wesleyan University Press, 1992 [1986]), p. 3.
2. Barbara Ehrenreich. Foreword to Volume 1 of Klaus Theweleit, *Male Fantasies* (Minneapolis: University of Minnesota Press, 1987 [1977]), pp. ix–x.
3. Gilles Deleuze and Félix Guattari. *A Thousand Plateaus: Capitalism and Schizophrenia,* translation and Foreword by Brian Massumi (Minneapolis: University of Minnesota Press, 1987).
4. Mauricio Aranguern Molina. *Mi confesión: Carlos Castaño revela sus secretos* (Bogotá: Oveja Negra, 2001 [8th edition, 2002]), pp. 108–9.
5. Amelia Moore. "Stark Relief: The Place of Shock and Stimuli in a Diary of Constant Terror." Essay for the seminar "Anthropology of the War Machine," Columbia University, fall semester 2002.
6. Carlos A. Leon. "Unusual Patterns of Crime during *La Violencia* in Colombia," *American Journal of Psychiatry* (May 1969): 1564–75; 1566. These figures coincide with those provided by Rodrigo Guerrero and, independently, by Mauricio Rubio, showing a marked increase in national homicide rates beginning in the mid-1980s, reaching around 85 per 100,00 in the early 1990s. See the Inter American Bank, *Hacia un enfoque integrado del desarrollo: Etica, violencia, y seguridad ciudadana,* 1996, Washington, D.C.,

pp. 59, 77. For Cali, Guerrero presents a rate as high as 180 in 1993, the last year shown in this publication.

7. German Guzmán Campos, Orlando Fals Borda, Eduardo Umaña Luna. *La Violencia en Colombia: Estudio de un proceso social,* Volume 2 (Bogotá: Tercer Mundo, 1964), pp. 62, 79–115, 158–61.

8. Jean Genet, p. 90.

9. Jean Genet, p. 263.

10. Gonzalo Sanchez and Donny Meertens. *Bandoleros, garnonales y campesinos: El caso de la violencia en Colombia* (Bogotá: El Áncora, 1984), p. 160.

11. Elsa Blair Trujillo. *Las Fuerzas armadas: Una mirada civil* (Bogotá: CINEP, 1993), p. 73. Daro. *Betancur and Marta García: Matones y cuadrilleros* (Bogotá: Tercer Mundo, 1990), pp. 74–5. Elsa Blair Trujillo presents figures (p. 67) for the composition of the defense forces in Colombia during the years 1948–1953: National police (incorporating municipal and departmental), 25,000 men; army, 15,000; navy, 3,200; air force, 1,200; and "illegitimately constituted forces," 5,000.

12. Sanchez and Meertens, p. 160.

13. Betancur and García, p. 135.

14. Betancur and García, pp. 94–6.

15. Betancur and García, pp. 76–7.

16. Roland Barthes. "Deliberation," in Susan Sontag (ed.), *A Barthes Reader* (New York: Hill and Wang, 1977), p. 491.

17. Robert A. Sobieszek, *Ports of Entry: William S. Burroughs and the Arts* (Los Angeles: Los Angeles County Museum of Art and Thames and Hudson, 1966), p. 51.

18. Walter Benjamin. "Theses on the Philosophy of History," in *Illuminations* (New York: Schocken, 1968), p. 263.

19. Carlos Medina Gallego. *Autodefensas, paramilitares y narcotrafico en Colombia: Origen, desarrollo y consolodación. El Caso "Puerto Boyacá."* (Bogotá: Editorial Documentos Periodisticos, 1990), p. 177.

20. Alfredo Rangel Suarez. *Colombia: Guerra en el fin de siglo* (Bogotá: TM Editores, 1998), p. 189.

21. Amnesty International Index: POL 10/001/2001; www.Amnesty. org, p. 1.

22. These figures are for the first ten months of 2001. Robin Kirk, "Humanization of Conflict and Human Rights in Colombia." In *Colombia: Conflict Analysis and Options for Peace-Building; Assessing Possibilities for Further Swiss Contributions* (Bern: Swiss Peace Foundation, 2002).

23. As described by Robin Kirk, Humanization of Conflict."

24. WOLA (Washington Office on Latin America), www.wola.org. June 11, 2002, p. 1.

ACKNOWLEDGMENTS

One of the first casualties of injustice is the abuse and eventual loss of a person's name. It is thus a grim and ironic gesture to acknowledge the nameless who fill these pages; all these estranging initials, these P's and these M's, these L's and these X's, reminiscent of a confidential psychiatric study or maybe a police dossier. If it is true that historical construction should be devoted to the memory of the nameless, I can only hope that the bearers of these initials have emerged in the previous pages in ways that convey, if not their fullness as real, named people, then at least the remarkable quality of life they uphold. When justice emerges in Colombia, which will have to be part of a worldwide change in economics and ethics, then we will see, as if by magic, these initials open like flowers into the full and real names that their initials hold dormant, In place of death lists we shall have life lists and beyond that an end to all lists.

Then there are the extraordinary people closer to home who commented on early drafts. I wish to thank Anna Blume, Marcus Boon, Marc Chernick, Maria del Rosario Ferro, Oscar Guardiola, Gabriel Izquierdo, Adam Isacson, George Marcus, Amelia Moore, Rachel Moore, Joey Slaughter, David Stoll, Julie Taylor, and Peter Lamborn Wilson.

Daniela Gandolfo of Columbia University got me thinking about diaries in new ways through her comments on Roland Barthes' comments, and Annette Bicker, Sarah Rushforth, and other writing students pushed me further in that direction in our seminar on the diary-form held at the California Institute of the Arts in Los Angeles.

Deirdre Mullane went way beyond what is normally expected of a literary agent, and my New Press editors, Andy Hsiao and Jonathan Shainin, were remarkably patient and smart, making everything seem not only easy but exciting.

Todd Ramón Ochoa, who studies African religion in Havana, Cuba, was my traveling companion for the first week. With his generosity and complete openness to all the people we met, he made me see myself as much as the situation in unexpected ways.

Much of my research the past decade was made possible by the generosity of the Harry Frank Guggenheim and the John Simon Guggenheim foundations.